SOMER
-SET
DEVON
DORSET

THE PIG

THE PIG

500 MILES
of
FOOD
FRIENDS
and
LOCAL LEGENDS

THE PIG

Introduction

A lot has happened in the three years since we published our first book. We have opened three more hotels and, of course, we've all had a global pandemic to contend with. Our ops director Tom has definitely had his work cut out, so it's certainly not been boring! Our Pigs now reside in every county across the south coast of England, from the rugged Atlantic coastline of Cornwall to the vineyards and hop fields of Kent – close to 500 miles, if you take a meandering route from Pig to Pig. Inspired by guests who had linked up stays at two or three Pigs as the basis for a staycation road trip, we thought it would be interesting to make this journey from county to county – and Pig to Pig – in book form. Chef director James wanted to showcase the unique produce and flavours of each area, while also introducing the cast of fascinating characters that make up the broader Pig family.

Since we opened the first Pig in 2011, we have sought out (or in some cases, they've sought us out) an incredible collection of artisans, who have become a big part of our story. The immediate 'family' is our core team of close to 1,000 employees who work tirelessly to ensure that every guest has the best time. Equally as important are the connections forged with our wonderful local suppliers. It's a two-way relationship that plays an essential part in your experience with us. It's why – we hope – each Pig has its own unique atmosphere and flavour. And it's not just the brilliant farmers, fishermen, foragers and winemakers who we rely on, but a whole myriad of other creative people... everyone from Ollie's seed suppliers, through to George, Cornwall's surfing instructor to the rich, the famous and – most importantly – to the Pig guests! They all play their part.

So through the pages of this book, you will get to know a few more of our most valued artisan friends. You will meet some of Judy's favourites: from Hilly, in Exmoor, who creates the most beautiful lampshades out of silk saris, to dreadlocked Charlie and his lovely wife, Katy, who make our vintage-style parasols from a stone barn near Penzance. You will hear more about co-founder David's landscaping talents and you will read about the wonderful, ever-youthful octogenarian Rachel, who grows kiwis, among other things, in her organic garden near The Pig-on the Beach. When she has a bumper crop, she simply brings them to the back door of the kitchen in exchange for supper in the restaurant, which feels like a great way of doing business. (Let's hope HMRC isn't reading this!)

Who wouldn't be captivated by the story of James and his band of fellow scallop divers a little way along the coast at Lyme Regis, who spend 80 minutes at a time underwater collecting these fascinating creatures? When I think of the endeavour and skill involved in getting a single scallop from the seabed onto the plate, via our kitchen, where it is cooked simply with thought and care, all in a matter of hours, my admiration for both fisherman and chef goes through the roof.

There is a recurring story here of new generations of farming families reinventing themselves, of mixing old skills and new ideas. The super-talented winemaker Rob Corbett from Castlewood has transformed the family plot from a typical small mixed Devon farm to one that now grows some of the best grapes and makes some of the best wine in the county. Or Tom Calver from Westcombe Dairy in Somerset, who had no intention of getting involved with the family farm, but now produces serious award-winning cheddar, an absolute favourite of mine. Not to mention the story of Giles at Longland Farm. Kamil, now our head chef at The Pig-in the South Downs, first came across him herding geese through a local village and promptly put in a big Christmas order. One thing led to another, Kamil started ordering duck too, and now we are one of Giles's biggest customers.

We also wanted to take you photographically behind the scenes to see a little of the life and people 'backstage' at The Pig: the unsung heroes of hospitality. You may well get to know the front-of-house team during a stay at one of our hotels, but it's this crew, who you may never see, who keep the show on the road. They are the troops who ensure the linen is in tip-top order, your bed is made properly, the washing-up is done with care and attention, and much more besides.

I proudly now have three generations of my own family involved in the business. Of course Judy still works with her customary passion and eye for detail to create our much-loved interiors. Our son Ollie runs the ever-enlarging kitchen-garden operation, and his partner, Jo, our 'queen bee', has embarked on a much more serious commitment to beekeeping and honey production. She is assisted by our four-and-a half-year-old granddaughter Stephie, our youngest beekeeper, while her three-year-old brother, Dougie, is garden 'helper' extraordinaire! Meanwhile, our other super-talented son, artist Will, has created the hotel crests and road map illustrations in this book. Actually, I suppose I could claim five generations rather than three, as Nan's recipe for rice pudding, hand-scribed by my mother and featured at the beginning of our first book, is still a firm favourite on the menus.

Guests are always fascinated by the history of the buildings that become our hotels and how we find them, so we have attempted to give a potted history of each one (don't expect Pevsner-level detail). Most are listed by Historic England, including the most important, architecturally speaking: The Pig-at Combe, which is Grade I-listed, placing it in the top two and a half per cent of all listed buildings. They all have intriguing pasts, and whatever their backstory and future life, for now we are happy to be the guardians of a very special collection of buildings.

Happy browsing, cooking and gardening. I hope you enjoy meeting our extended family here. So on behalf of David, Judy, Tom, James, Ollie and indeed the whole crew, thank you as always for your continued support.

Robin x

THE NEXT GENERATION.
A HANDFUL OF OUR KITCHEN APPRENTICES – WHO SAID MILLENNIALS ARE FLAKY AND CAN'T APPLY THEMSELVES? THIS CROP WILL BE AT THE FOREFRONT OF RESTAURANT COOKING BEFORE WE KNOW IT.

01

SURFERS, SMUGGLERS AND LOBSTERS

CORNWALL

AT HARLYN BAY

G
LOBSTER
Shed
SANDY
SHOE TAP
DIRTY BEACH
TOWELS

1636
HM

Robin: This moody house was a real find, full of atmosphere, stories and rugged attitude. We've owned a home nearby for nearly 20 years and had walked along the sunken road within a hundred metres of this house many times, but it was so perfectly hidden we didn't know it existed. I had always said I wouldn't create a Pig in Cornwall as it's too far from London, but while we try to resist such instincts in favour of more considered evaluation... it was just love at first sight with Harlyn House. So, although we're not allowed to have favourite Pigs, this building is definitely close to our hearts.

LAID-BACK, RUGGED AND BEAUTIFUL – WHEN YOU'RE DOWN ON THE BEACH AT HARLYN BAY, THE REST OF THE WORLD CAN GO HANG

Our Cornish Pig only came about because of a chance encounter. Robin happened to meet a member of the family that then owned Harlyn House, who explained that they were looking to sell. The Millar/Alkens were only the third family to own the house in its 600-year history, and it's easy to see why – you really wouldn't let it go in a hurry. It's one of the oldest and, we think, most dramatic stone houses in the county, originally a farmhouse dating from the 15th century, which got grander over the centuries as more intricate architectural details were added. Its name is said to come from the Cornish for 'the place by the water'. Sitting on a breathtaking stretch of the north Cornish coast, overlooking Harlyn Bay, the house is handsome, tough and more than a tad romantic: you just know it's weathered storms and scandals, and maybe turned a blind eye to a bit of dodgy dealing back in the day (some say there was a smugglers' tunnel from the house to the beach).

There's something about this area – its remoteness, its rugged beauty – that creates a maverick, independent spirit that suits us down to the ground. Some of our favourite chef friends, like Rick Stein and Paul Ainsworth, are down the hill in Padstow, not to mention many of the country's oldest fishing families and loads of brilliant growers and producers. The food scene has become really exciting – the fish is as fresh as it gets, and the climate means that lots of produce thrives when it might struggle anywhere else, so the kitchen really has something to play with. It's a close-knit community of people who really care about the future of this corner of England, and we love being part of it.

We might be biased, but Harlyn Bay, even by Cornish standards, is special: from the hotel you just stroll down to the sandy beach, where gulls wheel overhead as surfers catch the waves and that particular Cornish cocktail of characters go about their business. Come evening, families are packing up their kit, surfers are heading out for the last ride of the day, walkers are finishing a stint on the coast path, a bunch of mates are grilling fish on a campfire, and the odd harem-panted truth-seeker is doing a sunset downward dog. It's laid-back, rugged and beautiful – when you're here, the rest of the world can go hang.

'WHEN THE SEA IS LIKE GLASS AND DOLPHINS ARE ALL AROUND THE BOAT, THEN IT'S THE BEST JOB IN THE WORLD'

Johnny Murt, FISH BUOYS, PADSTOW

Fishing runs in the Murt family's veins. Johnny supplies us with the most delicious fresh lobster and crab, and is a familiar face down on the quay in Padstow most days, in his yellow oilskins, landing his haul and loading up the van with his dad, Maurice. His brother Martin and their cousin also fish off their own day boats, his auntie helps out with the crab picking and processing, and his wife, Cam, handles all the paperwork. 'My granddad died three years ago now, but back when I bought this boat, he came out of retirement so he could come to sea with me. He'd be fine for two days, get moody on the third, we'd have an argument on the fourth, then he'd come back because he just wanted to be at sea. It was great fun for me. Now I feel like my dad's filling that role.'

Although he was brought up on the sea and bought a boat with his brother at 18, Johnny spent years living a very different life, studying marine biology and aquaculture in the UK and USA, before working as a fishing liaison officer. 'I was meeting with fishermen and politicians all over Europe, taking a bollocking on behalf of the government because we were going to be putting in marine protected areas, then going out on the beer with them and smoothing it all over. It was good; it was fun. But being around fishermen, in Zeebrugge or Peterhead, listening to their stories, it just made me miss fishing. So I bought a boat and came home.'

Despite the stresses of running his Fish Buoys business, he doesn't regret it: 'I just love the fishing. It's the really nice days, that's what keeps you at it, when you experience something that probably no one else does in their job, that level of enjoyment. When the sea is like glass and there are dolphins playing all around your boat, then it's the best job in the world. I see seals, porpoises, pretty big sunfish.' A normal fishing day starts at about 5.30/6am when Johnny sets off on his boat, the Rachel May. The furthest he'll go is about 13 miles from Padstow, working strings of 20 pots, hauling them and rebaiting. He'll be back by 5pm, loading up and making deliveries – the Lobster Shed included. 'I love my food and we're very spoilt that we have so many good restaurants around here. I like to think I'll use my studies at some point. I've always got ideas for projects, but I don't want to take away from my fishing time. That's what I enjoy the most.'

LOBSTERS, LOBSTERS, LOBSTERS...

After a morning on the beach, what's better than a table in the fresh air, with a view of the sea, some lobster and chips to tuck into, blues on the sound system, one bottle of rosé down and another on the way? The Lobster Shed is our very own mash-up between a New England lobster shack and a beachside Greek taverna, but 100 per cent Cornish.

There's plenty more than lobster on the menu – loads of local fish and shellfish, steaks, padron peppers, char-grilled vegetables – but we have to say the lobster is the star, especially with head chef Adam's thermidor sauce, using the local Cornish Gouda, and our best thrice-fried chips. For every lobster we serve, we donate £1 to our friends at the National Lobster Hatchery. The work they do is incredible, investing in world-class research into lobster breeding and, most importantly, working with designated local fishermen like Johnny to fish sustainably to maintain the local lobster population.

The Hatchery produces about 50,000 baby lobsters a year, releasing them into the waters around Padstow. As our friend Clare, who works there, says: 'It's not just about saving lobsters, it's about saving these coastal communities.' So the fact that we serve lots of lobsters ironically helps the conservation efforts of the Hatchery. It's the perfect sustainable food story.

Before we opened at Harlyn Bay and were developing the menus, Robin wanted to include a lobster thermidor. We really wanted ours to stand out so Adam, head chef here, came up with a version that has three times more cayenne and mustard, to really give it a punch. We also add a concentrated lobster stock, cream and, in our opinion, one of the finest cheeses in the UK – vintage Cornish Gouda. To make sure it got on the menu, Adam went to Robin and Judy's home and served them a traditional thermidor and a Harlyn thermidor side by side... and the rest is Lobster Shed history!

lobster harlyn

Put the court bouillon ingredients in a stockpot and bring to the boil, turn down to a simmer and continue cooking for 5 minutes before you put the lobster in. We use an electric stunning machine first, currently considered the most humane method of killing lobster. If you are cooking at home, you can buy frozen lobsters from a fishmonger who uses this method before freezing.

Cook for 6 minutes (for every 100g over 500g add a minute to the cooking time). Remove from the pan with tongs and immediately plunge into iced water. Put 500ml of the court bouillon into a clean pan.

Once the lobster's chilled, take off the claws. Split the body in half and discard the intestinal tract and the stomach (small and bag-like near the mouth, generally with undigested food inside). Add the roe and brains into your 500ml court bouillon. Remove the claw and knuckle meat, rinse the head cavity and place the meat back in, avoiding getting the rest of the meat wet. Add the claw shells to the pan. Bring to the boil, lower heat and continue cooking until the liquid is reduced to a thick syrupy stock.

Chop the shallots very finely and place in a large pan. Tie the tarragon stalks together with fine string and add to the pan (you can tie the other end to the saucepan handle so you're not chasing string around the pot). Add the wine and reduce until only a third is left; add the fish stock and reduce in the same way. Soften the butter and mix to a paste with the flour. Remove the tarragon from the pan and discard.

Reduce the heat and add the flour and butter paste to thicken the sauce. Simmer for 3-5 minutes to cook out the flour. Stir in the cream and reduced lobster stock. Add the mustard powder, paprika, Worcestershire sauce and cayenne pepper to taste – it needs to be intense! Finish with half the grated cheese. Check for seasoning and add more if you need it. Finely chop the fresh herbs and add to the sauce just before serving.

Top the lobster with sauce and the remaining cheese. Place under a medium hot grill to heat through and melt the cheese. Serve straight away.

Serves 2

- 1 x 500g live lobster

For the court bouillon

- 200g celery, sliced
- 200g carrot, sliced
- 200g onions, sliced
- bouquet garni: 4 sprigs thyme, 4 sprigs tarragon and 3 bay leaves tied in a muslin cloth
- 3.2 litres water
- 220ml dry white wine
- 100ml white wine vinegar
- 40g rock salt
- 4 garlic cloves
- 3 teaspoons peppercorns

For the Harlyn thermidor sauce

- 2 banana shallots
- 3 stems tarragon
- 300ml dry white wine
- 300ml fish stock
- 20g salted butter
- 20g plain flour
- 60ml double cream
- 1 tablespoon reduced lobster stock (see method, left)
- 1 teaspoon mustard powder
- 1 teaspoon smoked paprika
- a scant teaspoon Worcestershire sauce
- ½ teaspoon cayenne pepper
- 100g grated vintage Gouda
- salt and pepper
- fresh herbs such as chives, parsley and tarragon (50g in total)

However many crab or prawn cocktails you've had, we honestly think that the sweetness of Cornish spider crab adds something pretty special to this classic combo. If you want to serve it in the head, make sure you boil the shell with bicarbonate of soda and let it dry fully, just to keep it nice and clean. And if you happen to be near a rocky Cornish beach, there's no better place to enjoy it.

spider crab cocktail

Serves 4 as a starter

- 1 spider crab, weighing 1-1.5kg
- sharp, heavy-bladed knife
- crab picks
- heavy-duty tea towels
- rolling pin

For the Marie Rose sauce

- 200g mayonnaise
- 70g tomato ketchup (we use Rubies in the Rubble)
- a scant teaspoon Worcestershire sauce
- a few drops of Tabasco
- small pinch celery salt
- 1 tablespoon brandy
- a good squeeze of lemon juice

It's more humane to kill the crab before cooking. A live crab may shed its legs when boiled, and killing the crab beforehand prevents this from happening. Flip it upside down and pull open the flap on the underside. Pierce the crab through the centre point with a small sharp knife or skewer and move it from side to side. This will kill the crab instantly. The legs will go floppy but may still move and twitch with nerves.

Put the crab upside down into rapidly boiling water, bring back to the boil then start timing – 12 minutes per kilo (for example, a 1.5kg crab will take 18 minutes to cook). Once cooked, remove the crab from the pan. Rinse the crab to remove any excess protein and allow to cool fully. Remove the legs and claws and set aside. Pull the body and shell apart and scrape all the brown meat out of the shell into a bowl. Remove the pointed gills from the central part of the body and discard; cut the body in half. Pick all the flesh out of the honeycombed centre into a bowl. Wrap the legs and claws one at a time in a tea towel and crack open with a rolling pin or hammer. A sharp thwack should do the job. Pick out all the meat.

For the sauce, mix everything together in a bowl with a whisk or fork – this can be kept in the fridge for up to a week.

To serve, mix half of the white meat into the brown together with the Marie Rose sauce. Put into the clean dry shell, then place the remaining white meat on top.

Oily fish are synonymous with Cornwall, and mackerel is one of our real favourites. It's so versatile – smoked, grilled or baked are all great options, but if you're lucky enough to catch one or buy it straight off the boat, then don't hesitate to try it cured. Mackerel and gooseberries are made for each other: it's one of those combinations that, once tasted, you'll be in love with for ever.

cured mackerel

Serves 4 as a starter

- 4 fresh mackerel fillets
- coarse salt
- a sharp filleting knife

For the gooseberry, elderflower and shallot dressing

- 100g gooseberries, thinly sliced
- 100ml elderflower cordial
- 1 banana shallot
- 1 small garlic clove
- zest of 1 lemon, finely grated
- salt and pepper
- 100ml rapeseed oil

The day before you want to cook this, place the sliced gooseberries in the cordial.

Freeze your mackerel fillets then partly defrost to use. Lay flesh-side-down on a bed of coarse salt for 10 minutes. Take them out of the salt, rinse, pat dry then lay on a clean cloth and leave to dry a little more for 5 minutes or so. Carefully peel the skin away from the flesh and dice the fish as finely as possible.

Using a sharp knife, chop the shallot very finely and put into a small bowl. Grate the garlic against a Microplane (if you don't have one, use a fine, sharp grater). Add to the shallot with the lemon zest and a pinch of salt and pepper. Now add the oil and cordial and mix everything together.

Add the fish and stir to make sure the dressing coats it (the acidity of the lemon helps to cure the fish). Leave for a minute before spooning onto the plates. Distribute the gooseberries and shallots evenly, and drizzle over the dressing.

Tim Marshall's Porthilly oysters are salty, sweet mouthfuls of deliciousness and luckily for us they're close by, just on the other side of the Camel Estuary, along from Rock. Tim really does all the hard work for us – all we need to do is open them and pair with something that shows them off. Classics are classic for a reason and shallot vinegar with oysters requires so little work – just a really good vinegar.

porthilly oysters

Allow 2-4 oysters per person

- oysters
- tea towel
- oyster knife
- coarse salt

For the kea plum shallot vinegar

- 2 banana shallots
- kea plum vinegar, enough to cover the shallots (we use Jonathan Gould's cider vinegar with kea plum from Grampound, not far away from us, but a cabernet sauvignon vinegar is a good alternative)

Dice the shallots as finely as you can. Place in a sieve, quickly rinse under hot running water then leave to drain. Combine with the vinegar and leave for 24 hours before using.

Push the knife into the 'hinge' of the shell and twist it to open the shell. Take the knife under the oyster to release it. Turn the oyster over in the shell and check for any stray pieces of shell. To serve, place the shells on small mounds of damp, coarse salt. Serve with the shallot vinegar, lemon wedges and Tabasco.

9PM: RUNNING THE PASS, DINNER SERVICE

MainPass
DR
2x SML Smoked Salmon
1x SML Tomatoes
1x SML Asparagus
1x 10oz Sirloin Steak
2x Red Mullet
1x Whole Dover Sole
OFF THE BONE
1x Pollock
1x Lamb
2x Broccoli & Walnuts
1x New Potatoes
1x Chips
1x Garden Pickle Salad
TABLE: 20 / 6C
Restaurant
Away
KATIE

OUTDOOR SHOWER, ANYONE?

There's something about this part of Cornwall that makes you want to do things a bit differently. We've always loved our huts and cabins at the Pigs, used as bedrooms, treatment rooms or outdoor dining rooms. But at Harlyn we fancied designing some supersized shepherd's huts as bedrooms – or shepherd's huts on steroids, as Robin likes to call them. Super-cosy, but with plenty of room for a sitting area and a proper bathroom, they were built by a great little company called Plankbridge near Dorchester, run by master hut-maker Richard Lee and his partner, Jane. Oh, and we added a cheeky, private outdoor shower just for fun.

'I TAKE THINGS TO ADAM THAT HE'S LITERALLY NEVER TASTED'

Lynn Freer Ash, FORAGER

There are no such things as weeds to Lynn Freer Ash. 'There's more stuff you can eat than you can't, it's just about looking all the time and constantly learning,' she says. A free spirit if ever there was one, with her festival looks and off-grid lifestyle, Lynn has been foraging the north Cornish coastline for the past decade, and loves sharing her finds with Adam, head chef at Harlyn, and the rest of the kitchen.

'I took the Pig chefs out a couple of months back,' she says, 'and we found 22 different edible plants. I often take things to Adam that he's literally never tasted!' She reels off the names of some of her regular pickings – sorrel, wild carrot, sea beets, sea fennel, campion, plantain, sea thistle – explaining as she goes the nuanced tastes and medicinal properties of each, like a be-hatted, tattooed professor of plants. 'Have a taste of this – scurvy grass. It's full of vitamin C; quite peppery, though. And this – ribwort plantain. It tastes like mushrooms.'

Lynn started foraging by accident about a decade ago. She had moved to Cornwall with her young daughter to help look after her mum. Every day she would walk the four miles along the rugged stretch of coast from Treyarnon to Booby's Bay with her dog. Gradually she started to tune in to what was growing all around her, becoming increasingly interested in the natural medicinal properties of everyday plants, with their anti-fungal and anti-inflammatory powers. 'Picking is like meditation,' she says, 'and it's just about Googling things, looking carefully at pictures, tasting things, learning more. Everywhere is blooming.'

Podding broad beans is endlessly satisfying – the feel of your thumb running along the edge of the pod and then that perfect pop revealing the emerald green jewels inside their velvet overcoat. When they're fresh and in season you really don't need to do much to prepare your beans, leaves and pods – they're tender and delicious enough just as they are, uncooked. A local soft fresh cheese and plenty of minty dressing on a warm spring day is really pretty spectacular.

broad bean & porthleven mozzarella salad

Serves 4 as a starter or side dish

- 150g broad beans, podded (shelled weight)
- a few broad bean leaves
- 400g fresh young broad beans in pods
- 2 x Porthleven mozzarella balls, roughly torn
- salt and pepper

For the garden mint dressing

- 50ml white wine vinegar (infused with 6-8 leaves mint)
- 2 tablespoons Dijon mustard
- 100ml rapeseed oil
- 8-10 leaves mint, finely chopped
- a little honey or sugar to taste if needed

For the dressing, infuse your vinegar with mint at least 2 weeks in advance. Place the bruised mint into a jar with the vinegar, seal and leave for 2 weeks.

On the day it's needed, remove the leaves and mix the minty vinegar and mustard to a smooth paste. Whisk the oil into this and finish with the mint. (Otherwise blend the vinegar and mustard in a small spice grinder, add the oil and mint and blitz.)

Depending on the vinegar you use and your personal preference, you might want to add a little sugar or honey to take the acidity down a notch.

Blanch the podded broad beans for 1½ minutes, drain into a sieve, run some cold water over them, then pop them out of their skins. Pick the leaves off the stalks. Finely slice the young beans in pods.

Combine in a bowl with the mozzarella, salt and pepper and the mint dressing. Toss together and put onto your plates. If you have any cornflowers to hand, add a few petals on top.

In our first summer at Harlyn, head kitchen gardener Andy produced a bumper crop of everything in the fruit cage, so we wanted to base a whole pud around it. Berries, currants, zesty curd and crispy sweet pastry – everything good and all in one place. The best part is when you cut into the tarts and the curd and juices spill out, oozing sweet and sharp goodness.

fruit cage tartlets

To make 6 tarts

(You'll need 6 x 10cm non-stick tart cases, greased)

- 125g unsalted butter (plus extra for greasing)
- 90g icing sugar
- 250g plain flour (T55 if you have it!)
- pinch of salt
- 65g whole egg

For the lemon thyme curd

- 60ml lemon juice
- 3 sprigs lemon thyme, bruised
- 100g whole egg
- 60g egg yolk
- 50g caster sugar
- 100g unsalted butter, cut into pieces

Fruits for the tart

We're lucky to have fruit cages at all our properties, so we have a bounty of lovely fresh berries and currants, but use whatever you fancy

- 500g soft fruits, such as redcurrants, whitecurrants, raspberries, strawberries (regular and Alpine), blueberries, gooseberries

For the sugar syrup

- 500g water
- 500g sugar
- 8 sprigs lemon thyme

For the pastry, cream the butter and sugar in a food mixer until fluffy. Add the flour and salt and mix to a fine crumb. Gradually add the egg and mix on the slowest speed. Remove and bring together by hand. Wrap in clingfilm and chill.

Heat the oven to 180°C, 160°C fan (350°F), Gas Mark 4. Allow the pastry to soften a bit and sprinkle lightly with flour. Roll out on a lightly floured surface as thinly as you can. Using a saucer, cut out circles that are at least 1.5cm bigger than the tins. Ease the pastry in and try not to get any air trapped. With a small ball of spare dough, gently press around the edge of the cases. You can leave excess over the edge as it can be trimmed later. Double up clingfilm larger than the tin, position over the pastry, fill with baking beans and wrap. Bake for 15 minutes.

Unwrap the clingfilm, remove the beans and return to the oven uncovered for 10 minutes.

For the curd, heat a pan of water and place a metal bowl over, leaving space between the bowl's bottom and the water. Add everything except the butter, stirring all the time so it doesn't catch. Whisk until thick then remove the thyme. Take off the heat and add the butter. Cool and chill.

For the syrup, bring the water, sugar and thyme to the boil, take off the heat, sieve and allow to cool.

Slice the strawberries and gooseberries and halve the raspberries and large blueberries. Leave the currants whole; add fruits to the syrup.

To serve, take a small plate and dollop a little blob of the curd in the middle – use this to stop it from sliding around. Half-fill with curd. With a fork, select a nice range of fruit and place on top of the curd. Drizzle some syrup around the outside of the tartlet, but take care as you don't want that lovely crisp pastry going soggy! Garnish with edible petals.

'WE WERE ON THE FT'S LIST OF THE WORLD'S 50 BEST FOOD SHOPS. NEW YORK, PARIS, MILAN... PADSTOW!'

Ross Geach, PADSTOW KITCHEN GARDEN

There can be few farms in England with as lovely a view as Trerethern. Overlooking the Camel Estuary, with the ancient Saint's Way running along the bottom of the fields, the land has been farmed by the Geach family for seven generations. And it's here that Ross runs Padstow Kitchen Garden, on a corner of the 100-acre family farm that his mum and dad, Ron and Sonia, still run.

We've known Ross for years, from when he was head chef at Rick Stein's cafe – 'I started washing up there when I was 15,' he says – so when we need extra veg on top of what we produce in our own kitchen garden, he's our first call. His stuff is top-notch and he really understands how chefs think and what they need. 'A little bit of everything, that's how we do it,' he says, talking us through the midsummer crop. 'A mix of lettuces – cos, red butterheads, green frisée, bionda, baby gems. Then we do tomatoes, herbs, padron peppers, peppers, cavolo nero, Tenderstem broccoli, kale, loads of kalettes, cauli. And I've got three polytunnels a mile away full of courgette flowers. To have The Pig on my doorstep is amazing, I just text Adam, tell him I've got a load of really good chard or whatever, and he says, "Bring it over." It's really collaborative; we'll chat in the winter about what new stuff to try.'

Both Ross and his dad talk with pride about the land their family has tended for 200 years: 'The farm cost £50 – a lot of money back then,' says Ron. 'The soil here is exceptional,' explains Ross. 'I did a soil science course, and we got it tested to make sure the pH levels were right. I don't use phosphates, we add sand from the estuary, which has loads of minerals from the river and the sea: it's exported all over the world, it's so good.' Ross always loved the farm: 'I spent loads of time as a child out here with my granddad. We'd help out with picking and we thought we were just having fun, but actually we were doing a job, learning without realising it. When I was young, me and Dad would both enter the Padstow fruit and veg show. It got really competitive – who'd win what between me or him! We used to get the cup every year.' Now the plaudits come from loftier places. 'We've got this tiny farm shop, selling our own stuff, other local producers' food and mum's cut flowers. And we were in the Financial Times's list of the 50 best food shops around the world, along with all these really fancy places. New York, Paris, Milan... and Padstow!'

Kelvin, our pastry supremo for all The Pigs, has been doing a lot of research into old English puds. This one, which sounds so romantic, and just a bit naughty, is a lemon jelly flavoured and coloured with saffron. Highly coloured foods were very popular in the 17th century, made in a fancy mould then turned out, decorated with small edible flowers and maidenhair fern, and traditionally served with homemade biscuits. Saffron is a highly prized part of Cornish culture and history, and is used in cakes and traditional Cornish saffron buns, which you can find on our breakfast tables – ours is grown by Brian and Margaret Eyers on the Roseland Peninsula.

cornish moonshine

Serves 4

- 2 unwaxed lemons
- 600ml water
- 115g caster sugar
- 15g leaf gelatine
- 10-20 saffron strands
- Tarquin's Dry Gin (this is optional, for an extra-special adults-only version; omit the equivalent amount of water from the recipe)

Using a veg peeler, remove the zest from the lemons. Place the water (remember, if you're going to add gin, reduce the water by the corresponding amount), sugar and the pared rind into a pan and gently bring to the boil.

Turn down to a low simmer for 15 minutes, then take off the heat and leave to cool. Squeeze out the lemon juice (you'll need 80-90ml) and strain into a bowl.

Place the gelatine in a jug of cold water and let it soften. Pass the syrup through a fine sieve and set aside.

Put a small amount of the syrup into another pan.

Add the saffron and return to a gentle heat to allow it to release its colour. Once the colour has developed, remove from the heat and add the softened gelatine. Stir it in to make sure it dissolves completely.

Add the lemon juice and the rest of the syrup and mix everything together. If you're adding gin, now's the time!

Transfer to a large jug and pour into a jelly mould or individual glasses, making sure the saffron strands are divided evenly between the glasses. Put into the fridge and after 30-40 minutes give the mix a stir to bring the strands up from the bottom to 'float'. Chill in the fridge for at least 2 hours.

CORNWALL

IF WALLS COULD TALK

When Judy started to imagine how she wanted Harlyn's interiors to look, she was thinking of this ancient stone house on dark and stormy nights, not just in the blaze of summer. So she came over all mean and moody and worked with a new palette of dark shades, luscious velvets and richly patterned papers and fabrics. The result is a house that you sink into, with its Delabole slate walls, flagged floors, rugged wooden doors leading off lamplit hallways, roaring fires and ancient stone friezes, such as this one from the 1630s, featuring sea beasts. You get a feeling that if walls could talk, these could definitely tell you a tale or two...

'SURFING IS ABOUT LIVING IN THE MOMENT. THAT'S ALL YOU CAN DO'

George Stoy, GEORGE'S SURF SCHOOL

Our friend George is one-part surfing genius, one-part philosopher. He and his team of coaches at George's Surf School have helped lots of our guests to venture into the waves since we opened, and his thoughtful and super-knowledgeable approach makes everything seem possible. 'Surfing is living in the moment,' he says. 'That's all you can do. It won't work if you try to dominate the water or impose your will on it. It's about listening and feeling. Feeling the water, feeling the wave, being connected to the board under your feet. It's play for adults.'

George's first sporting love was skiing – which he also instructs – but from childhood he also loved to surf and gradually it took hold of him: 'It became a bit of an obsession. I started doing it more and more, and started teaching more. I noticed that people were different when they came out of the water; there was clearly a therapeutic aspect to it and I got fascinated.' At the time, George was working as a stockbroker in London, but would race down to Cornwall to surf whenever he could. 'Each time I went back I realised I was making better decisions and had more clarity. It's what's called "blue health" – the benefit of being in the water and the ocean. I didn't understand it at the time, I just knew it made me feel better.'

So George went on a bit of an odyssey, surfing all over the world, from Hawaii to Sydney to Europe, and learning about different approaches to coaching in the water. 'Surfing is still largely first generation in the UK, so those learning are often the first in their family to try it. But what makes it rewarding is when someone really wants to learn, to be vulnerable, to go outside their comfort zone and to improve. I love enthusiasts, so I look them in the eyes and recognise a bit of myself and think, "This is great, we're going to get on."' He even put his two-year-old daughter on a board recently for the first time: 'She's a real water baby: she had no fear and just stood up!'

George has lots of friends locally involved in the food scene, as chefs or growers, and is fascinated by the connections between their world of green health, and his of blue health. 'They're like the guardians of everything,' he says. Having surfed all over the world, he says when he first went to Hawaii he felt faintly embarrassed, that people there might think our surfing was a bit second-rate, but in fact they were fascinated by the Cornish surf scene. 'What travelling teaches you is the value of home, and there's something magical about Cornwall. It's not just the waves, it's the backdrop and the horizon. There's nowhere else I'd want to be.'

Sometimes food just tastes better on the beach. Sun going down, beer in hand, coals turning from red to grey, it's hard to go wrong if you've got some great-quality fish to throw on there. Martin Murt (lobster Johnny's brother) turns up at the back door of the kitchen at least once a week bearing a crate of painfully fresh fish that was in Harlyn Bay less than an hour before. One of the top prizes in that mixed bag is always his red mullet. We barbecue it whole in the main kitchen and serve it with a simple butter and brown fish stock sauce – but cooked on an open fire, it takes some beating. Either way, the fish should be crispy on the outside, hot and moist in the centre, and should come away from the bones nicely.

beach barbecued red mullet

Serves 4

- 4 small red mullet, scaled and gutted
- a little good rapeseed oil
- salt and pepper
- 4 garlic cloves, finely chopped
- 4 sprigs rosemary, leaves removed and finely chopped

Light your barbie. Pile up loads of charcoal, get it burning well and when the coals have turned from red to grey, you're ready to go. Combine the oil, salt, pepper, garlic and rosemary to a paste in a spice grinder or pestle and mortar. Score the fish skin – about 0.5cm deep – and rub the paste over the fish, inside and out. Place on the barbecue, turn after 4-5 minutes then cook for a further 4-5 minutes.

If you're cooking at home on a gas or electric barbecue, get the temperature up to around 250°C (480°F) then allow it to cool slightly to around 180°C (350°F). Place the fish on the barbecue; turn after 4-5 minutes and cook for a further 4-5 minutes.

If you want to do this in a normal oven, just place the fish on a wire rack with foil underneath and use the same method as above, but maybe give the fish a minute longer on each side.

Butcher Philip Warren over in Launceston has been one of those blessings we didn't fully appreciate when we started buying from him. His meat is second to none and the rump caps are stunning – tender and packed with flavour. Wood smoke, beef fat and sea air is a combination that just always hits the spot.

Charcoal pit rump cap

Light your barbecue. Pile up the charcoal in a sandy hollow, get it burning well and when the coals have turned from red to grey, you're ready to cook. Oil and season the beef, place it fat-side-down on the barbecue and cover with foil. Turn the meat every 2 minutes, replacing the cover each time. Cooking time should be around 15-18 minutes per pound for rare/medium rare, but to be more accurate, it's best to test with a digital thermometer – you want a core temperature of 46°C (115°F). Rest for 5 minutes then slice across the grain. Perfect with a hunk of baguette from our friends over at Da Bara Bakery.

If you're cooking at home on a gas or electric barbecue, get the temperature up to around 250°C (480°F) then allow it to cool slightly to around 180°C (350°F) then follow the instructions above.

Always check that barbecues are allowed on the beach and make sure you clear up your mess afterwards!

Serves 5

- 1 x 900g rump cap
- some good-quality rapeseed oil
- salt and pepper

HARLYN BAY TO GITTISHAM - 103 MILES

02

GREEN AND PHEASANT LAND

DEVON

AT COMBE

TURKEYS
"NORFOLK"
BLACK
Devon
The Shire of Great Seamen
Part of Cornwall
BRITISH RAILWAYS

The Best Exotic Marigold
Bug Hotel

Robin: Definitely the poshest of all our Pigs (or should I say architecturally the most impressive: it's Grade I-listed, don't you know), Combe House has truly arresting views and is home to some rare colonies of bats who live happily alongside us in the roofs and outbuildings. We felt it important not to over-restore the house, so while it's a bit grander than the others, it's more faded grandeur than anything else. The previous owners, Ken and Ruth, had run it as a good country-house hotel for a number of years but perhaps hadn't landed on the right formula for it to be a robust business in more recent times. We took the opportunity to add a dozen new bedrooms by converting the perfectly formed stable-yard quad behind the main house, and these have become some of our most popular rooms. The best bit for me at Combe is the cellar, full of atmosphere and intrigue. We often hold wine tastings and the odd dinner down there – ask to take a look on your next visit.

OLD BISHOP ODO, WHO FIRST OWNED THIS LAND, SURE KNEW HOW TO PICK A GOOD SPOT

It's just over 100 miles from Harlyn Bay to the Otter Valley near Honiton – and a very different world. After Dartmoor, with all its bleak beauty and drama, the landscape eases back into deep wooded valleys and rolling hills, thatched roofs and medieval churches, pottering pheasants and signs for cream tea. Devon is the most bucolic of English counties, and we feel lucky to have landed up in one of its loveliest corners. Combe means wooded valley and this place certainly lives up to its name – as you drive up the long, long track from the village of Gittisham, you catch your first glimpse of this Grade I-listed star, all honeyed stone and Elizabethan tall chimneys. As Robin likes to say, 'Old Bishop Odo, half-brother to William the Conqueror, who once owned this land, sure knew how to pick a good spot.'

Originally part of a much larger estate (the current owners, the Markers, are our very friendly neighbours), Combe House passed through a series of grand and occasionally grumpy families over the centuries – with the odd tantrum, disinheritance and royal intervention thrown in. One of the best-known families was the infamous Putts, of Tom Putt apple fame. Tom was an unpopular landowner, prone to rages and feuds, but he did build The Folly, one of our favourite bits of Combe, so we'll forgive him. There's so much we love about this house – it's a world all of its own, with views as far as the eye can see towards the Mendips and the Blackdown Hills, huge old cedars in the garden, one of our loveliest kitchen gardens – and there's some stiff competition – and even its own farm down the track.

It's so perfect here that when The Pig team looking after the house during lockdown were given the option to go back home, they all decided to stay! The food scene combines the best of land and sea: the Combe chefs have a cornucopia of organic produce to work with, grown by local producers who've farmed this land for centuries and newcomers who are building their own dreams, plus some of the country's best seafood. And anywhere that produces the legend that is Devon Minnow – our unique Bacchus wine – is definitely a special place for foodies and wine-lovers.

9AM: PHEASANT SHOOT, COMBE ESTATE

COMBE
ESTATE
DAMSON
GIN

The Pig-at Combe sits on a 4,000-acre estate, with pheasant and partridge roaming the fields – if you're up early, you'll see them pottering up the drive and in the kitchen gardens. Once the season opens, estate manager Justin's shoots supply us with ample pheasant. We use it in so many ways – from hearty stews to pheasant and lentil soup – but this dish, with its strong autumn and winter flavours, is a real classic.

combe pheasant breast with mush(y)rooms

Serves 2

For the mushroom purée

- 250g chestnut mushrooms
- 1 banana shallot
- 1 tablespoon rapeseed oil
- 30g unsalted butter
- 20g Demerara sugar
- 40ml cabernet sauvignon vinegar
- 50ml double cream

For the red wine sauce

- 1 banana shallot
- 1 teaspoon olive oil
- 150ml beef or chicken stock
- 100ml red wine
- ½ tablespoon red wine vinegar
- 1 sprig rosemary
- 25g unsalted butter

For the pheasant

- 2 pheasant breasts
- salt and pepper
- 2 sprigs fresh thyme and rosemary
- 50g salted butter

Finely slice the mushrooms and shallot. Heat the oil and butter in a pan, add the mushrooms, let them cook until soft then add the shallots. Cook gently until the pan is almost dry, turn down the heat, add the sugar and stir. Cook until the sugar is dissolved then add the vinegar.

Reduce the vinegar until it's evaporated then add the cream. Taste for seasoning and adjust where needed. While it's still warm pulse in a blender to form a purée.

For the red wine reduction, chop the shallot as finely as possible. In a pan, heat the oil over a medium flame and sauté the shallot without colouring. Add the stock, wine, vinegar and rosemary and bring to a simmer. Cook until the volume of liquid has reduced by half. Remove from the heat, add the butter and stir until melted and combined. Pass the sauce through a fine sieve and check the seasoning. Keep to one side until ready to serve.

Heat the oven to 200°C, 180°C fan (400°F), Gas Mark 6.

For the pheasant breasts, leave the skin on and season both sides with salt and pepper. Over a medium heat, sear the breasts skin-side-down in a heavy-bottomed pan. Once the skin is crispy, flip over and add the herbs and butter. Continue basting over a low heat for 3-4 minutes till cooked. Leave to rest for 5 minutes (the meat should be slightly pink when carved).

Warm the red wine sauce and mushroom purée. Arrange on your plates with the pheasant and steamed greens.

O'THREE
O'THREE

'OUR SCALLOPS COME OFF THE BOAT AND ARE AT THE PIG WITHIN A FEW HOURS'

James Moyle, SCALLOP DIVER

Down in Lyme Regis, a young fisherman by the name of James Moyle has become our go-to scallop man. James is part of a small team of independent fishermen who club together to rent a little boat: a Holton 24, named Petrisha Ann (although he has just bought his own boat, Grey Mist). Most mornings they'll leave the Cobb as the sun rises and pootle five miles out to sea. They'll then strap on their scuba gear and dive down into the depths of the English Channel in search of scallops.

'We take it in turns to dive at around 20-30 metres for anything up to 80 minutes,' says James. 'We try to work along the reefs, but scallops also have a habit of living in muddy ground. Providing we have at least 50 centimetres of visibility, we're usually good to go.' He adds stoically: 'You can't always see your outstretched hand, but you can certainly feel your way along a rockface easily enough. On the flipside, in summer, visibility can reach 10 metres and it suddenly becomes more like the Caribbean, with corals and pink sea fans.'

Until a year or so ago, James was an arable farmer, but when a position on the boat became available he says the stars aligned. 'My main passion is surfing and I have a degree in agriculture management so, for me, it really is the best of both worlds.' James dives twice a day when conditions allow: severe cold is fine, but if the sea is too rough the visibility worsens, meaning the scallops just have to wait. The trouble is, we find James's hand-dived scallops far better than the alternative: 'Sustainability is the main benefit of diving for scallops,' he says. 'There's no bycatch, and no damage done to the seabed. We're very selective when we're down there, we know what an in-size scallop looks like, and if we do pick any undersize ones, we'll put them straight back in.

Which means we're allowed to dive in protected areas where trawling and dredging is banned.'

In the UK, the majority of scallops are still caught by dredging, and overfishing is rife. 'When scallops are dredged, they end up being pulled through grit and sand for about half an hour, so people do say dredged scallops are grittier,' says James. 'Ours are much fresher, too. Whereas a large dredger might be at sea for a week, ours come off the boat and they're at The Pig within a few hours.' Takes some beating.

James Moyle is affectionately known to the Combe chefs as Goldenballs, so prized are his hand-dived scallops from Lyme Regis Bay! They're some of the best-quality scallops around and, to be honest, the less we do to them, the better. Preservation of the bay and seabed is hugely important to us so we have scallops on the menu only when they're in season. The sea veg is foraged by our chefs from around the Beer area, a couple of bays west of Lyme Regis.

scallops with wild garlic butter

Serves 4

For the wild garlic butter

- 30g wild garlic leaves
- a good pinch of Maldon sea salt
- 100g unsalted high-quality butter, softened

For the scallops

- 12 scallops
- 1 tablespoon rapeseed oil
- a pinch of salt
- sea veg or lemon wedges to serve

Heat the oven to 200°C, 180°C fan (400°F), Gas Mark 6.

Wash and pat dry the wild garlic leaves and add to your blender with the salt (when not in season, use a couple of garlic cloves). Add the softened butter and blitz at a high speed until well incorporated.

Put in a tub to firm up in the fridge (any left over can be cut into cubes and frozen for a future dish).

Heat your grill.

Wash the scallops and pat dry on a kitchen towel. Drizzle some rapeseed oil and sprinkle salt on them and put back in their shell. Cook in the oven for 3-4 minutes, add a couple of small nuggets of garlic butter to each shell and finish under the hot grill for a further 2 minutes or so.

We serve the scallops in their shells over some wet rock salt to keep them stable, with a combination of fresh or pickled sea veg to finish the dish and bring some acidity. If you can't get your hands on any sea veg, just put them on a plate with a wedge of lemon.

We're big fans of the two ps – pickling and preserving. They're a great way to keep our local flavours, even out of season. Plaice – we get ours from the day boats out of Beer – is a wonderfully flavoursome fish. It's best cooked simply, with preserved lemons and sweet and sour peppers adding a gorgeous zesty kick.

day boat plaice, sweet & sour peppers

Serves 4

For the pickled lemons (make in advance)

- 2 unwaxed lemons
- 300ml white wine vinegar
- 150g caster sugar
- lemon leaves (if you can get them)
- 3 sprigs lemon balm or lemon verbena

For the sweet and sour peppers

- 3 red peppers
- 100g red onion
- 2 garlic cloves
- 150ml olive oil
- 30g caster sugar
- 90ml white wine vinegar

For the day boat fish

- 2 whole plaice (each weighing around 600g; 1 fish between 2 people)
- salt and ground white pepper
- 25g salted butter, softened
- juice of 1 lemon
- 2 teaspoons baby capers

Place the lemons in the freezer until firm but not solid. Using a very sharp knife, slice them as thinly as possible. In a pan, heat the vinegar and sugar and simmer for 20 minutes. Remove from the heat and add the leaves and herbs; allow to cool. When cooled, pour over the sliced lemons and cover with a lid. Allow to sit for at least two days before using.

Peel the peppers with a veg peeler, remove the seeds and slice into strips. Thinly slice the onion and garlic. Warm the oil in a pan over a medium heat, add the peppers and onions and cook until soft. Add the garlic and sugar and stir to dissolve. Add the vinegar; taste and add more sugar if you need it. Chill until you're ready to serve.

Heat the oven to 200°C, 180°C fan (400°F), Gas Mark 6.

Season the skin on both sides with salt and ground white pepper and brush on some soft butter. Heat a frying pan until it's fairly hot, then add 2 tablespoons of the pepper-preserving oil. Add the fish presentation-side-down (which for us is the white side).

Continue cooking over a medium heat for around 3 minutes until lightly caramelised. Flip over and caramelise on the other side. Once coloured on both sides, place on a tray with the cooking oil and squeeze over the lemon juice.

Place in the oven for 4-5 minutes. Check if the fish is ready: pierce with a skewer in the thickest part. If there's little or no resistance, remove from the oven and leave to rest for 3-4 minutes before serving. After the fish is cooked you can use the same pan to quickly warm up the peppers and add the capers. Adjust the seasoning with salt and pepper.

The pickled lemon slices can be draped across the fish and some of the pickle juice used to increase acidity in the dish.

'DAN CAME DOWN TO THE FARM AND LEFT WITH A WEEK'S WORTH OF TOMATOES AND COURGETTES'

Harry and Emily Boglione, HAYE FARM

Harry and Emily Boglione are flying the flag for the next generation of young British farmers, despite being relative newbies to the game. After becoming disillusioned with city life in 2013, they moved to Devon to explore the idea of living off the land.

'When Emily and I started out, one of our main frustrations was that the big-business farms were maintaining a profit but not doing anything positive for the environment,' says Harry. 'Meanwhile, the permaculture movement has good intentions but is considered a bit hippyish and not hugely productive. We wanted to create a farm that was a profitable business, but that would demonstrate how we can improve the current state of nature, while creating great products.'

So they bought Haye, a 90-acre farm in need of a little TLC. From the outset, the plan was to plant hedgerows, woodland and wildflower meadows to increase biodiversity. At the same time, they began growing fruit and vegetables – rather successfully, as we soon discovered, although no one was overly surprised, as Harry hails from our friends the green-fingered family behind London's Petersham Nurseries.

'As we began growing more and more vegetables, we started looking for customers with a similar ethos to ours,' says Emily. 'The Pig-at Combe had just opened, so we invited Dan and a few of the chefs down to the farm for a tour and some lunch and we got along famously. They left with a week's worth of tomatoes and courgettes, and it's gone from strength to strength ever since.'

As has the farm. Today, chickens, lambs, pigs and cows (Red Ruby Devons, Aberdeen Angus and Herefords) move happily between the verdant pastures. 'With "mob grazing", we're trying to mimic what was once the natural behaviour of these herbivores,' explains Harry. 'This kind of short-duration, high-intensity grazing gives the more vulnerable species of vegetation the opportunity to grow and set seed. And the more variation in the animals' diets, the more flavour in the meat.' Emily adds that mob grazing also helps to build soil carbon, crucial in their quest for a carbon-negative farm. 'Regardless of climate change, it's sensible for a farmer to sequester as much carbon in to their land as possible. The more carbon in the soil, the better the microbiology, which means better growth rates for our livestock and vegetables.' They taste pretty good, too.

If head chef Dan's not foraging, then it's highly likely he's making pasta and gnocchi – he loves it. We use whichever foraged mushrooms are in season, or we pick a good selection of our own, grown in our epic mushroom house here (when you're cooking at home, any wild mushrooms will work). If you're a bit daunted by the thought of making gnocchi, just give it a go – it's a great alternative to pasta. This is a gorgeously rich, autumnal treat, and the Old Winchester grated cheese finishes it off perfectly.

ricotta gnocchi with zero-mile mushrooms & chard

Serves 4

- 250g ricotta
- 85g whole egg (2 small eggs)
- 40g heritage flour such as spelt, emmer or einkorn (if you can't get heritage flour look out for ancient grains or a decent wholegrain)
- 150g '00' flour
- a good pinch of salt
- a pinch of grated fresh nutmeg
- a little coarse semolina for rolling
- 150g mixed wild mushrooms
- 1 tablespoon rapeseed oil
- salt to taste
- 2 garlic cloves, crushed
- 20–30g butter
- 25–30ml dry white wine
- 100g rainbow chard
- 20g Old Winchester cheese, finely grated
- black pepper

Put the ricotta and egg into a KitchenAid or similar mixer and, using the whisk attachment, mix on a medium speed till the egg is incorporated and the ricotta looks smooth.

Change the attachment to a paddle and add your dry ingredients, mixing slowly. Once the ingredients come together, stop the machine and, dusting your hands with some flour, work the dough for a minute by hand.

Spread a little coarse semolina onto the work surface and roll the dough into a sausage about 2.5cm high. Sprinkle some more semolina over the top, cover with a cloth or bowl and leave to rest for 30 minutes in the fridge.

Once rested, cut into 2.5cm pieces and blanch in salted boiling water for 3 minutes – they're ready when they start to float. Drain, return to the pan and keep warm.

Wash the mushrooms if they need it and gently dry on a kitchen towel. Leave uncovered on a tray in the fridge until you're ready to cook. In a pan, warm the oil and add your mushrooms with some salt and crushed garlic. Once they start to caramelise, flip them over and add a knob of butter. Reduce the heat so the butter doesn't burn.

When the mushrooms are almost done, add a splash of wine to the pan to deglaze, then add your gnocchi. Turn the heat down to low, add more butter if needed and some more wine to bring it all together.

Wash and roughly chop the chard; add to the pan when the gnocchi are hot. Finish off with the grated cheese and black pepper.

The mulberry dates back to Tudor times, and happily we have a beautiful old tree in the grounds here. No one knows exactly how old it is, but it's likely to be almost 100. The fruit is somewhere between a raspberry and a blackberry and can vary in colour and sweetness. You rarely find them in the shops so you can use other berries instead. This is a delicious warming pud that goes with cream or ice cream, but we love it with good old Bird's custard!

mulberry sponge pudding

Serves 4

(You'll need 4 x 200ml pudding moulds)

- 100g unsalted butter, softened
- 100g caster sugar
- 80g whole egg (2 small eggs), lightly beaten
- 100g self-raising flour
- 30ml buttermilk or double cream
- a little extra butter or vegetable oil
- 4 dessertspoons hedgerow jam or similar
- 150g mulberries (or raspberries or blackberries)
- 20g caster sugar

Beat the butter and sugar until light and fluffy in a KitchenAid or food mixer. Slowly add the egg, trying not to split the mix. If it starts to separate, add a little of the flour to bring it back before adding more egg. Add the flour in four stages, beating slowly. Add the buttermilk or cream and finish mixing by hand.

Grease the moulds with butter or veg oil, place a dessertspoon of jam in the bottom of each mould, then fill to two-thirds of the way up with the sponge mix (using a piping bag is the easiest way!). Place in a steamer, cover the pan and cook for 30-35 minutes.

Put the berries in a small pan with a splash of water and the caster sugar, then gently heat to a simmer to soften the fruit.

Once the sponges have steamed, carefully turn out of their moulds and spoon the berries on top. Serve straight away with Bird's custard.

This is the epitome of a garden dish, perfect for a light lunch or starter on a warm summer evening. It's super-simple and can be whipped up in minutes. We use our homegrown peas at Combe but (whisper it) we think it tastes pretty good with frozen. Basil oil to finish is the killer secret ingredient and a great alternative to the more usual mint pairing.

chilled pea soup with garden basil oil

Serves 4 as a starter

This is a delicious stock and can be used for many dishes, so it's always good to have some in the freezer.

For the vegetable stock (make in advance)

- 4 medium carrots
- 4 sticks celery
- 1 large white onion (or 2 small)
- 1 medium leek
- 850ml water
- 20g soft herb stalks (such as coriander and parsley)
- 40ml lemon juice
- 5 peppercorns
- 125ml dry white wine
- a good pinch of salt

For the basil oil

- 15 large basil leaves
- 80ml cold pressed rapeseed oil

For the soup

- 400g fresh or frozen peas (shelled weight)
- 400ml vegetable stock
- 4 dessertspoons crème fraîche

Cut the vegetables into large cubes and put in a large pan with enough water to just cover them. Bring to the boil and simmer for 8 minutes. Add the herb stalks and boil for an extra 2 minutes. Take off the heat and add the lemon juice, peppercorns, white wine and salt.

Leave overnight and pass through a sieve the following day.

For the basil oil, prepare a pan of boiling salted water and a separate bowl of iced water. Take the basil leaves and blanch for 1 minute in the boiling water. As soon as the minute has passed, drain and place into ice-cold water till cold. Drain and pat dry on kitchen paper.

Add the basil to a small blender or spice grinder and pour over the rapeseed oil till it reaches the same level as the top of the leaves (around 100ml).

Blitz on a high speed for 2-3 minutes then let it chill over ice.

You can pass this through a muslin cloth or leave as it is if you want a more rustic look.

For the soup, pod the fresh peas and blanch in salted boiling water for 2 minutes; refresh in iced water and drain. If you're using frozen peas, they're fine to use straight from the freezer (and this helps keep the temperature down if you're serving the soup straight away). Chill.

Put the peas in a bigger jug blender, add the chilled vegetable stock and cover to the top of the peas. Start blending on low then gradually increase the speed. You might need to adjust the amount of stock you're adding, depending on how thick you want your soup. Check the seasoning.

When you're ready to serve, pour the soup into a chilled bowl, add a dollop of crème fraîche and drizzle a little basil oil on top. Garnish with whichever herbs and petals you prefer – we use fennel tops, chives, borage and nasturtiums.

Red Ruby beef is the best-known Devon breed, and Alastair and Philip David at Darts Farm are two of the most experienced butchers we know. Carpaccio is a great way to preserve beef – most people assume it's difficult to prepare but it actually demands minimal effort for maximum impact. We serve it with a local hard cow's cheese, Curworthy Belstone. It's based on a traditional 17th-century recipe and aged for a further two months so it has a really rich flavour. The truffle makes the dish – be generous, it's worth it!

darts farm red ruby beef carpaccio

Serves 4 as a starter

- 400g beef fillet
- salt and pepper
- 50ml good-quality cold pressed rapeseed oil
- zest and juice of 1 lemon
- 100g rocket
- 20g fresh truffle (if you can get it, otherwise use 50ml truffle oil instead of the rapeseed oil, making sure it's not made with artificial flavouring, plus a little rapeseed oil to sear the beef)
- 80g hard cheese, shaved – we use Curworthy Belstone from north Devon

Ask your butcher for the freshest piece of beef fillet (or you can use sirloin) and season lightly all over with salt and pepper.

Heat a heavy-bottomed frying pan with a little oil and sear the beef briefly, ensuring all the sides are sealed. Remove from the pan and allow to cool.

When cool, wrap tightly in clingfilm to form a sausage shape and freeze. Once frozen, let it thaw a little (this will make it easier to slice). Using a sharp knife, slice as thinly and carefully as possible. Place the slices straight onto your serving plate and drizzle over half the rapeseed oil (or truffle oil if you can't get fresh truffle). Whisk together the rest of the rapeseed or truffle oil with lemon zest and juice, salt and black pepper, then dress the rocket leaves with it and spread around the meat. Shave over the fresh truffle and hard cheese to finish the dish.

There's nothing we love more than a good pork pie. This version, courtesy of Rob, senior sous chef at Combe, goes up a notch, using Darts Farm Duroc-cross pigs and served with rhubarb butter. Made with shortcrust, it's slightly easier than using the hand-raised hot water pastry method, so if you've never made a pork pie before, give this one a go – you'll feel a great sense of achievement.

rob's pork pie

Serves 8-10

(You'll need a 20cm loose-bottomed tin, 6cm deep)

For the pastry

- 125g salted butter
- 1 large egg
- 2 tablespoons ice-cold water
- 500g plain flour
- 1 teaspoon salt

For the rhubarb butter

- 200g trimmed rhubarb
- 50g unsalted butter
- 50g caster sugar

For the filling

- 1 banana shallot, finely diced
- 25g salted butter
- a good pinch each of nutmeg, salt, pepper
- 650g pork shoulder
- 50ml brandy
- 250g minced fatty pork
- 50g smoked streaky bacon (or lardons), chopped finely
- 1 tablespoon sage, chopped
- 1 egg yolk to glaze

For the jelly

- 100ml red wine sauce
- 200 ml water
- 3 bronze leaf gelatine

First make the pastry. Put your butter in the freezer till it's hard but not frozen. Whisk the egg with the water and put into the fridge till needed. Grate the butter. Place the flour and salt in your food mixer and, at slow speed, using the paddle, gradually add the butter (don't mix it too much; you want some chunks to add to the flakiness). Add the egg and water and combine. Knead briefly to bring it together and cover tightly in clingfilm. Let it rest in the fridge for at least 1 hour. Now make the rhubarb butter.

Slice the rhubarb as thinly as possible. Heat the butter in a pan until bubbling, place the rhubarb in the foaming butter and cook for 2-3 minutes, stirring constantly. Once cooked, pour into a sieve and keep the liquid and pulp separate. Place the pulp in the fridge. Return the liquid to the pan, bring to the boil quickly and add the sugar to taste. Reduce liquid by half, then chill. Blitz pulp in a blender and slowly add glaze. Chill until needed.

Now for the filling. Sweat the shallot in the butter and once it's soft (but not coloured) take off the heat and add the nutmeg, pepper and salt. Allow to cool. In a food processor, chop the pork shoulder with the brandy; mix with all the other ingredients (apart from the egg yolk). Heat a frying pan with a little oil, cook a tiny amount and taste (adjust seasoning if necessary).

Remove the pastry from the fridge and leave to soften slightly for 10 minutes to make it easier to manage. Cut one-third from the pastry to reserve for the lid. Flour the surface lightly and form the pastry into a ball; don't work it too much. Roll out to around 30cm and gently mould the pastry into the tin. Spoon in the prepared pork mix (the filling should come to the top).

Roll out the rest of the pastry to form a lid. It needs to be about 5mm thick and at least 1cm wider than the pie tin to allow enough to seal the edges. Lightly whisk the yolk and brush a little over the pie rim. Lay the lid on top of the filling and, using thumb and index finger, gently crimp the edges.

Make a hole in the centre to allow steam to escape. Use the remaining yolk to glaze the top twice and let the pie rest in the fridge for 30 minutes. Heat the oven to 220°C, 200°C fan (425°F), Gas Mark 7. Cook for 20 minutes then reduce the heat to 180°C, 160°C fan (350°F), Gas Mark 4 until the pie's internal temperature reaches 62°C (you'll need a digital thermometer). Remove from oven and allow to cool for a good half hour.

Now make the jelly. Warm the liquids together in a pan, add seasoning. Soak gelatine in cold water, when fully softened add to the hot liquid, stirring until dissolved. Once pie is cooled, make a hole in the middle of the pastry and pour in jelly slowly with a funnel. Chill to set.

FONSECA
PORTO

'WE LET THE WINE EXPRESS THE CHARACTERISTICS OF OUR LAND AND THE VINTAGE... THAT'S THE REAL SKILL IN WINEMAKING'

Rob Corbett, CASTLEWOOD VINEYARD

In 2016, Rob Corbett planted two hectares of Bacchus vines on the warmest, steepest, south-facing hillside of Castlewood Vineyard in south Devon. It was something of an experiment – in the 10 years they'd been making wine there he'd mostly stuck to Pinot Noir, Chardonnay and Pinot Meunier grapes. Which is perhaps why, on a rather inebriated evening at the annual Castlewood Wine Festival, he generously offered the Bacchus vines to Robin and his good friend and fishing mate, chef Mark Hix. The plan was to produce a wine that was exactly to our taste, that could only be served at The Pig and one or two of Mark's restaurants.

'Bacchus really lends itself to the English climate,' says Rob, who started planting grapevines on his parents' Axe Valley dairy farm in 2006. 'When we get a slightly underripe year, the grape will have a more floral nature: low alcohols, higher acidity, and you get that nice elderflower, hedgerow character. As it ripens further, you'll be going into the fruit spectrum, green and red apples. After that it becomes more tropical, perhaps with notes of stone fruit. It's an incredibly versatile variety that can really express itself.'

By the time the Bacchus vines in block HH (Hutson Hix) had matured, Rob says he wasn't sure if Robin and Mark would even remember their somewhat blurry conversation. Well, needless to say, they both did, and so the three of them, along with a couple of The Pig's sommeliers, met in the cellars at Castlewood – armed with a few of their favourite bottles – to discuss exactly what they wanted to achieve.

'The general consensus was that we wanted to produce something very different to the existing English Bacchuses,' says Rob. 'We are all quite classical in our tastes, leaning towards old-world winemaking techniques, which generally means less is more.' Of course, that's not the most economical approach to winemaking, but it has never been about that for Rob. Each year he produces no more than 2,000 bottles of Devon Minnow.

The wine has become a magnificent drop. Ageing in Burgundy barrels from Mersault gives it a delicate, slightly spiced flavour. Renowned wine critic Matthew Jukes wrote, 'I advise everyone in this land to drink this wine, it will reconfigure the Bacchus landscape forever.' We had to hide our blushes. 'We don't try to force the wine into a certain dimension,' explains Rob. 'We let it express the characteristics of our land and the vintage, and I think that's the real skill in winemaking.'

Robin and Mark named the wine after a 200-year-old local spinning lure that is notorious for catching salmon and trout. On their fishing trips, Mark usually brings the lunch and Robin the wine – so you can rest assured that these days there's a bottle or two of Devon Minnow chilling in the river.

FOOD ROCKS

03

VERY, VERY LOCAL VENISON

SOMERSET

NEAR BATH

THING 2

WESTCOMBE
TRADITIONAL SOMERSET CHEESEMAKERS
THE PIG
THE PIG

Robin: Hunstrete House, home of The Pig-near Bath, has nostalgic memories for us. When I first started my adventure into country-house hotels in 1986 as an uber-keen general manager at the famed Chewton Glen Hotel on the edge of the New Forest, the owner, Martin Skan, sent me off to look at some of the other hotels he respected. One of those was Hunstrete House, run by John and Thea Dupays. These were halcyon days for rather formal, privately owned country hotels with Michelin-starred food and quite a lot of fuss. Sadly, that model was not really sustainable, and many of those iconic hotels were snatched up in the 1990s by the ill-fated Von Essen group. It wasn't too long before Von Essen fell into administration, and its 20-odd hotels were again up for sale individually. The only one I really wanted at that time was Hunstrete House, built in lovely Bath stone, and in 2013 we were lucky enough to buy it. But that's not the only connection we have with the previous hotel. My co-director David and his wife Sue spent their honeymoon night there – as you can imagine, there have been years of leg-pulling over that particular fact!

ONLY IN SOMERSET WOULD A DAIRY FARMER HAVE INVENTED THE WORLD'S MOST FAMOUS MUSIC FESTIVAL. THE CHEESE ISN'T BAD EITHER

Mellow is the word for everything about Somerset – surely the only county in England where a dairy farmer would invent the world's most famous music festival, where cutting-edge galleries sit amid dreamy meadows, and one of the local herdsmen used to play with The Kooks. Oh, and the cheese, cider and cream aren't bad either. And you wonder why it's our kind of place?

Hunstrete House was part of an estate belonging to the Abbey of Glastonbury, dating from the early 1300s. In 1830, the then-owners decided that the medieval manor wasn't up to snuff and demolished it to build 'a mansion on a most grand and magnificent scale'. And they did. But best-laid plans and all that, the family ran out of money and all that now remains are the 'romantic ruins' – the five arches you can see from our gardens. Our house was known as The Lodge and is quite grand enough for us, with its elegant Georgian proportions, honeyed stone, courtyards and 30 acres of deer park – quite a sight to behold if you wake up in The Hide, one of our kitchen garden rooms.

This is a creative part of the world, and despite its relaxed demeanour, there's loads of energy and interaction between farmers, artists, musicians – and chefs. We go big here on hearty cuts of the best local beef and pork (that rich Mendips pasture makes for very happy cows). Then there's the venison, as local as it gets, and our own honey – we've got six busy hives and counting – plus a scarecrow that looks like it went to Glastonbury in 1989 and forgot to come home. Oh yes, we do like the odd party in this part of the world – on Glasto weekend some very tired, very inebriated, very famous bodies have been known to crash out on our sofas come the early hours. Rumour has it that Florence (of 'the Machine' fame) once practised her set in the garden at dawn, as the Pig team all peeked out of the upstairs windows. We couldn't possibly comment.

One of the things people enjoy most about The Pig-near Bath is watching the deer that roam freely in the 30-acre park surrounding the hotel. Of course, the herd requires management so we have a regular supply of venison, which we love to showcase on our menu. We use every bit of the animal so nothing's wasted – needless to say, there are a few pies and sausages in there. This is one of our favourite venison recipes: it's super-simple, allows the meat to speak for itself and shows off our garden herbs and beets.

hunstrete venison & beets

Divide the herbs and garlic between two pans and boil the beetroots separately in salted water until tender (around 30 minutes). Allow to cool and remove the skin (easily done by hand, though you might want to wear disposable gloves for the red beet). Cut into wedges or halves, depending on the size.

Heat the oven to 200°C, 180°C fan (400°F), Gas Mark 6.

Season the venison with salt and pepper and heat a heavy frying pan. Put the oil in the pan then add the venison – you're looking for a nice bit of caramelisation on the meat, so keep rotating it until this is achieved.

Now add thyme, garlic and butter to the pan. Baste the meat with the juices and place in the oven for 3-4 minutes. Remove from the oven, place on a plate, lightly cover in foil and allow to rest for 5-6 minutes before carving.

Meanwhile, add your beetroots to the pan then add the cooking juices from the resting venison. Reheat the beets so they take on the flavour of the meat.

Once the beets are hot, slice your venison and serve with the beetroots, greens of your choice and all the lovely cooking juices.

Serves 4

- 10 sprigs thyme
- 10 sprigs rosemary
- 4 garlic cloves
- 1 bunch golden beetroot (around 500g)
- 1 bunch red beetroot (around 500g)
- 4 x 200g pieces venison loin
- salt and pepper
- 1 tablespoon rapeseed oil
- 4 sprigs thyme
- 4 garlic cloves, crushed
- 50g butter

10AM: VENISON BUTCHERY

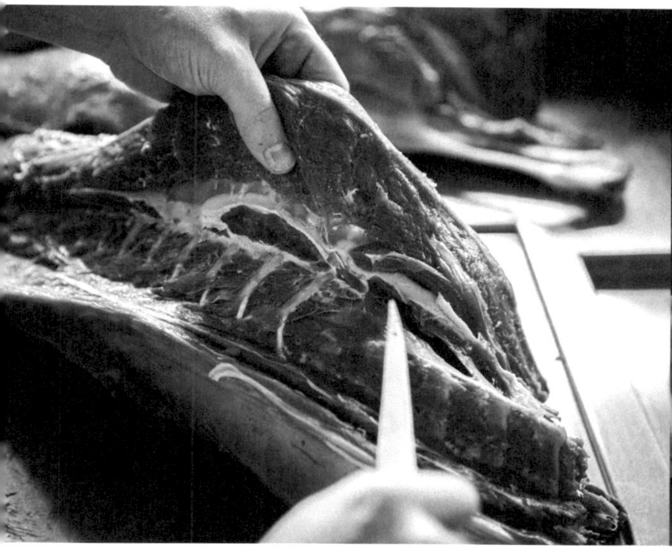
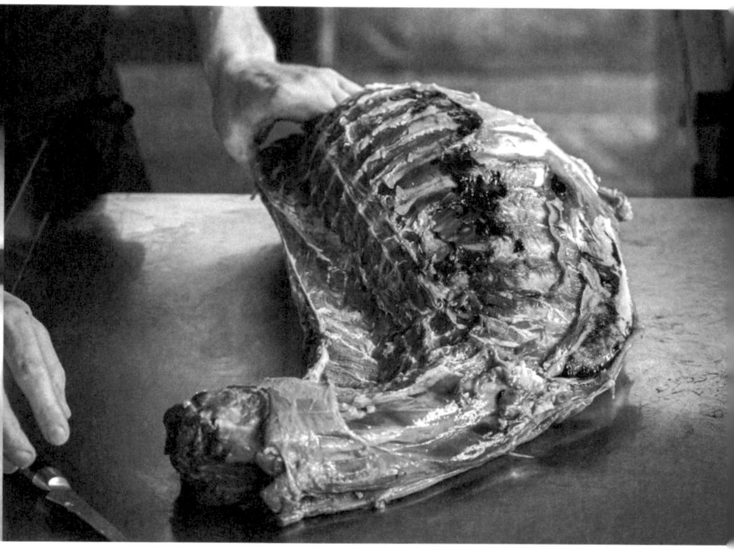

'DO I LIKE MY CHEESE STORE? I BLOODY LOVE IT! WOULDN'T YOU?'

Tom Calver, WESTCOMBE DAIRY

Tom Calver isn't just passionate about his cheese, he's obsessed – which is why English cheese doesn't get any better than Westcombe Cheddar (and why we're such big fans). Tom is on a mission to reclaim the word 'terroir', the French concept of place embedded in flavour: 'In dairy, it's wonderful to have this beautiful French word to explain the taste of a specific environment. What is it about this particular place that gives the cheese its flavour?' That particular place is Westcombe Dairy, not far from Bruton.

Originally a traditional dairy farm and cheesemaker (they've made cheese here since 1879), the farm turned to mass production methods in the 1970s, producing block cheddar for the wholesale market. But when milk prices hit rock bottom, Tom's dad, Richard, realised they had to add value, and so in the 1980s he decided to get back into traditional cheesemaking and started changing his farming methods. By 2002, Tom was working as a chef in London, but was miserable, so he decided to come home to help out. 'I'd vowed never to go into farming – dad worked far too hard – but I came home for a few months to help with marketing … and that was 20 years ago!'

Tom reels off fascinating nuggets of biochemistry cheese facts with infectious enthusiasm. For him there is no separation between managing the herd, caring for the land and making the cheese: they are all one. 'We're interested in quality, and if you go for that every single time, all the bits slot into place: the welfare of your cows; the quality of the pasture.' They have almost 20 different sorts of grasses, clover, chicory and legumes. 'If you start with the soil it goes upwards into the chain and the microbial diversity in our milk, which goes into the cheese and its flavour. We make cheese every day and each cheese tastes different.'

It's in the store that you really see the scale of Tom's ambition: it's a veritable cathedral of cheese, storing over 5,000 huge cheddars, in varying stages of mould-covered maturation, plus a couple of shelves dedicated to a 'library of cheese experiments'. Created by excavating into the hillside, it was inspired by a visit to Comté producer Marcel Petite. 'Do I like my cheese store? Oh, I bloody love it! Wouldn't you?' And the final touch: Tina the Turner, the robot Tom commissioned, which turns all the cheeses every 10 days or so. This frees up valuable time for Tom and his team, which includes Rob, a font of cheesemaking knowledge, and herdsman and ex-Kooks drummer Nick (whose Instagram, @herdsman_nick, reveals him to be a latterday Samuel Pepys of dairy farming). Never happier than researching old local recipes and experimenting with new ideas, they are total cheese-heads, the lot of them, and life (not to mention our Pig menus) is all the tastier for it.

We're not sure exactly when the poor old knobbly quince fell out of favour, but we're big fans and have some lovely old trees in the kitchen garden near Bath. Unlike apples and pears, the quince has to be cooked to reveal its fragrant glories – but one taste of this and you'll be a convert. The long, slow cooking time allows the honey and spices to really do their job, perfectly complementing the quince's delicate, perfumed flavour. Those Victorians knew a thing or two.

slow-roasted quince

Serves 4–6

For the quinces

- 4 quinces, cleaned of any brown down
- 1.8 litres stock syrup (made by heating together 700g sugar and 1.1 litres water until the sugar is dissolved; cool to room temperature)
- 200ml lemon juice (you'll need 4 large lemons)
- 70g runny honey
- 2 cloves
- 1 star anise
- 400ml dry white wine (whatever you have lying around – since it gets cooked out, it doesn't need to be anything special)

For the sponge

- 4 medium eggs, separated
- 160g caster sugar
- pinch of salt
- 160g pecans
- 30g plain flour

Peel the quinces, quarter and remove the cores. Place into the stock syrup and add the lemon juice. Bring to the boil and simmer for 40 minutes. Remove the quinces from the syrup and place in a baking tray (the cooking syrup can be kept and used with yoghurt and fruit). Drizzle over the honey and add the spices and wine.

Heat the oven to 180°C, 160°C fan (350°F), Gas Mark 4.

Cover the quinces with a piece of greaseproof paper and gently cook in the oven for 30 minutes. Then turn them over and ladle the juices on top (add more white wine if necessary). Return to the oven for a further 30 minutes. They should be soft and crimson coloured.

In a food mixer, whisk together the egg whites, 100g of the sugar and a pinch of salt to form a meringue; set aside.

Whisk the yolks and remaining sugar until the mixture is light and fluffy.

Heat the oven to 200°C, 180°C fan (400°F), Gas Mark 6.

In a mini food processor, grind the pecans finely, add the flour and blitz for a few seconds longer to combine.

Fold the meringue into the yolks gently so as not to knock the air out, followed by the pecan flour.

Spread onto a lined baking tray (around 22cm x 22cm) and bake for 15-18 minutes. Remove from the oven and leave to cool before cutting.

To serve, place a slice of the pecan sponge on a plate, put 3 or 4 quarters of warm quince on top of the sponge and drizzle the cooking liquor over the fruit. You can always add crème fraîche or ice cream.

It probably hasn't escaped your notice that we love a good pie at The Pig. But this one is slightly different from the meaty ones we usually serve – it's packed with veg from the kitchen garden and is light and wholesome. It can be made without dairy, so it's suitable for everyone. The vegetable filling can be adapted to what's in season and this mix, with the celeriac setting off the spinach and chard, is a firm favourite. Don't hold back on the spices – they're what help to make it so tasty. This one's even been known to convert the odd meathead!

spicy garden root pie

Serves 4–6

You'll need a 22cm x 26cm pie dish or 6 individual 16cm pie dishes

- 2 tablespoons rapeseed oil
- 1 large white onion, diced
- 3 garlic cloves, crushed
- 1 celeriac, peeled and diced (you want to end up with 600g flesh)
- 3 large carrots, diced
- 4 medium sticks celery, diced
- 1 tablespoon mild curry powder
- ½ teaspoon turmeric
- ½ teaspoon chilli powder
- salt and pepper
- 1 x 400g tin chopped tomatoes
- 120g fresh spinach
- 120g chard
- 320g puff pastry (shop-bought is fine)
- 1 large egg yolk

Heat the oil in a large saucepan and sweat the onion and garlic without colouring. Once it's fully softened, add the celeriac, carrot and celery.

Cook until everything has softened then add your spices and salt and pepper and cook for a few minutes more. Add the tomatoes and cook for 5 minutes (you may need to add a splash of water here).

Taste the mix and, if you're happy with the seasoning, add your spinach and chard – this will take just a minute to cook, so take care not to overdo it. Remove from the heat and allow to cool.

Heat your oven to 200°C, 180°C fan (400°F), Gas Mark 6. Once the mix has cooled, fill your pie dish (or dishes if you're using individual ones). Roll out the pastry to fit your dish (or dishes). Brush the inside edge of your dish(es) and egg-wash, then place the pastry on top, pinching it around the edge to seal. Using a pastry brush, egg-wash the lid well – this will give the pastry a nice glaze when it's cooked. Poke a hole in the middle to allow the steam to escape. Bake for 15-20 minutes or until the top is golden brown.

This risotto is spring on a plate. We're lucky to have lots of peas and beans in the gardens here, but if you can't lay your hands on a fresh crop, it's one of those recipes we can honestly say works just as well with frozen peas. People are often wary of making risotto and think they'll have to spend the whole evening chained to the stove, stirring away and ending up with a gloopy mush. But if you follow these steps we think you'll be converted. It's creamy but fresh and the addition of lemon at the end really cuts through the richness of the butter and cheese.

pea & broadbean risotto

Serves 4 as a starter

- 100g fresh or frozen peas
- 100g broad beans
- 30g butter or 2 tablespoons rapeseed oil
- ½ white onion, finely chopped
- 2 garlic cloves, finely chopped
- 250g arborio rice
- 75ml dry white wine
- 1 litre hot vegetable stock
- 50g butter, cut into small cubes
- 50g Duckett's aged Caerphilly from Westcombe Dairy (a mature, semi-hard cheese), or parmesan, grated
- juice of 1 lemon
- 10g fresh mint, shredded

Briefly cook the peas and broad beans in salted boiling water for 3-4 minutes, then drain and submerge in cold water to cool.

Melt the butter (or heat the oil) and sweat the onion and garlic gently over a medium heat – be careful not to colour it.

Once the onions are softened, add the rice and cook for a few minutes before adding any liquid.

Now add the wine; once it's well-reduced, begin adding the vegetable stock – one ladle at a time. Before adding the next ladleful, you'll need to cook the stock out so it's absorbed into the rice. Repeat this for the next 12 minutes or so until the rice is cooked.

Once the base is cooked, you can fold in your broad beans and peas. Add 50g butter and around half the grated cheese.

Using a wooden spoon, slowly work the butter and cheese into the risotto until it's creamy and rich. Adjust the seasoning with salt and lemon juice to your taste.

Spinkle the chopped mint and the rest of the grated cheese on top, and serve. Broad bean leaves and cornflowers make a pretty garnish.

QUEEN BEE JO (& OUR YOUNGEST BEEKEEPER)

Jo is our resident Queen Bee, the woman responsible for our burgeoning bee population and honey-making plans. Jo was part of The Pig right from the get-go. Originally from Poland, she'd been living in the East End of London: 'Ten years ago, I was working in a cafe in Brick Lane and doing other bits and bobs, but I was a bit lost. I came to the New Forest to get away and saw a sign for The Pig and thought it looked cool. So I went in and asked if they needed anyone.'

At first, Jo worked in the restaurant and was training to be a sommelier when she realised the garden was where she really wanted to be. So she joined the garden team in Brockenhurst and on her first day met Ollie, now our group head kitchen gardener, among the veg beds. Now, 10 years later, here they are – a couple, parents to Robin and Judy's grandchildren, Stephanie and Douglas, and in charge of all The Pigs' kitchen gardens and beekeeping.

'I got my first bees after about two years at Brockenhurst,' says Jo. 'I'd just started to get interested in honey-making. Then I went as head gardener to The Pig-on the Beach, and had about six hives there. I've done courses and taught myself a lot and we've produced bits and pieces so far, but now I'm ready to really go for it. We're going to be making our own honey at every hotel, and each will have its own distinctive taste. Most of the garden team are getting involved – it's exciting.' And Jo's trusty helper? Our youngest beekeeper, four-and-a-half-year-old Stephie: 'She loves it, especially using the smoker! I remember at Harlyn, we were opening up the hives and the honey just flows out. Stephie was catching it in her hands and just licking it off her fingers.' Sweet as honey.

This gorgeously creamy pudding is similar to panna cotta and makes the most of the delicious honey we've been producing here for the past few years. We're always looking for natural ways to sweeten puddings (rather than using processed sugar), so lucky for us that, thanks to our Queen Bee Jo, we now have six hives here, with more on the way. Somerset of course is famous for its milk and cream and we get ours from the Longman family, who've been farmers and cheesemakers in the Vale of Camelot for over two centuries.

honey & lavender

Serves 6

For the set cream

- 145ml whole milk
- 425ml double cream (we use Longman's)
- 125g runny honey
- 5 sheets bronze leaf gelatine

For the ice cream

- 1 litre whole milk
- 50g fresh lavender
- 200ml double cream
- 150g Trimoline (if you can't find it, use 110ml liquid glucose instead)
- 200g egg yolk (roughly 12 egg yolks)
- 150g caster sugar

For the set cream, gently warm the milk, cream and honey in a pan.

Submerge your gelatine in cold water and leave to soften. Remove the cream mixture from the heat, add the gelatine and stir gently to dissolve. Pass through a fine sieve. Pour into individual moulds or a shallow dish and allow to set for a minimum of 4 hours (even better, make it the day before).

For the ice cream, heat the milk and add the lavender. Cover with a lid and leave to infuse for at least 30 minutes. Pass through a fine sieve and add the cream and Trimoline or liquid glucose.

Return to the pan and gently heat through. Whisk together the yolks and sugar. Pour the warmed milk onto the egg mixture, whisking all the time. Return to the pan and warm over a medium heat, stirring all the time, until it reaches 82°C/180°F (you'll need a digital thermometer). Pass once again through a fine sieve, cool and place into lidded containers and freeze. Give it a stir every half hour or so for the first two hours to make sure it freezes evenly and stays smooth. There should be plenty for seconds, or keep whatever is left over in the freezer for another occasion.

'WE FEED ZERO SOYA TO OUR PIGS. I DON'T WANT TO BE RESPONSIBLE FOR DEFORESTATION OF THE AMAZON'

Josh Gay, NEWTON FARM

Revolutionaries can pop up when you're least expecting them. Just three miles away from us is the ancient village of Newton St Loe where Josh Gay's family have farmed the Duchy-of-Cornwall-owned Newton Farm for four generations. At just 26, and under the watchful eye of his dad, Hugh, Josh is now in charge of the day-to-day running of these 1,200 acres, a mixed farm of pigs, beef, sheep and crops. Head chef Jack is a fan, and the Newton Farm pork chop is a menu favourite, tender and full of flavour. 'Yes, we've got a good relationship with Jack and he knows I've got the environmental thing at heart,' says Josh, an ebullient character, striding around with piglets darting between his legs, and a 'Thing 2' tattoo on his calf (his twin brother, Will, who works in London, sports 'Thing 1').

Josh is making some big changes: 'I'm trying to farm in a regenerative way, reducing fertilisers, banning insecticides. If you improve the soil, you don't need to do very much, it does it all for you,' he says. He's being unduly modest, because Josh, like so many farmers, works around the clock, constantly trying to improve his methods. One of his major goals is to banish soya feed completely from the farm: 'We feed zero soya to our pigs. I don't want to be responsible for exporting environmental problems. Forty three percent of EU soya comes from Brazil and other South American countries and is used to fatten pigs and is fed to chickens, cattle and sometimes sheep. People told me I was going to lose growth rates and I said that's not the biggest issue for me, it's deforestation of the Amazon.'

Josh always knew farming was where his heart lay and studied agriculture at Reading. 'But you never stop learning. I listen to lots of podcasts, go to lots of meetings, I'm part of a grazing group.' All of which makes him sound a rather serious, studious sort – until he displays an earthy delight in describing how to judge the relative fertility of his very handsome bulls (including the very chilled Dave). But it's when he's zoning in on the details of regenerative farming with such knowledge (paddock rotation, why he's introducing chickens to follow on from the cattle to act as a natural parasite treatment) and plans for developing the farm shop, which his sister Kirsty manages, that you appreciate that British farming is in good hands. 'There's always more to do, but I genuinely think I'm going in the right direction.'

We think the tomahawk is the prince of steaks. Popular in the States (its name comes from the Native American word for a hatchet, because of the shape), you'll need to ask your butcher to prepare it but, trust us, it's worth it. Essentially a bone-in ribeye, it's astonishingly tender, with a buttery flavour thanks to the ribbons of fat that run through the meat. It's a big old steak, which makes it perfect for sharing, and there's no need for fancy sides – chips and a good salad will do it.

sharing longhorn tomahawk

Serves 4

For the steak

- 1 tomahawk steak weighing around 1.2kg
- 1-2 tablespoons rapeseed oil
- 50g butter
- 6 sprigs thyme
- 6 garlic cloves, crushed or sliced

For the salads

- 500g fresh mixed vine heritage tomatoes
- 10g fresh basil, shredded
- salt and pepper
- 1-2 tablespoons extra-virgin rapeseed oil
- 200g mixed baby leaf salad
- a little of your favourite salad dressing (we love Wild Island Bay & Juniper Balsamic Dressing)

For the chips

- 2-4 Maris Piper potatoes per person (depending on size), peeling optional
- vegetable or sunflower oil (enough for a deep fat fryer or chip pan)

Take the steak from the fridge at least 20 minutes before cooking to allow it to come up to room temperature.

Heat the oven to 200°C, 180°C fan (400°F), Gas Mark 6.

Heat the oil in a cast-iron frying pan and sear the steak until both sides are golden and well caramelised. Add the butter, thyme and garlic to the pan.

Place in the oven for 15 minutes (for medium rare). Remove from the oven and leave to rest in the pan, covered with foil, for 6-8 minutes.

While the meat's cooking, cut your tomatoes into halves or quarters and dress with torn basil, salt, pepper and the extra-virgin oil. In a separate bowl, place the washed salad leaves, drizzled with your favourite dressing.

For the chips, you'll need to start your prep the day before you plan to cook. Cut a small slice from one side of each potato and place the cut side down on the chopping board. This should mean the potato is now nice and stable and won't roll around as you chop it. Cut lengthways into 2cm slices, while keeping the potato together. Lay these down on their flat side and cut into chips 2cm wide. Place in a bowl and cover with cold water. Leave in the fridge overnight to release the starch.

Next day (eating day!), drain off the water and rinse. Steam the chips for 8 minutes using a double boiler pan. You want them to partly cook so you get that nice fluffy texture inside. Plunge them into cold water, then drain and lay them on kitchen paper to soak up any excess moisture. If there's too much water in them, they'll spit once they go into the fryer.

Heat the oil in a deep fat fryer (no more than one-third of the depth of the pan) to 150°C (300°F). For the second cook, blanch the chips in the hot oil for 8-10 minutes, then chill. When you're ready to eat, reheat the oil to 185°C (365°F) and fry till the chips are golden and crispy. Depending on the size of your pan, you may need to cook the chips in batches so they have room to brown evenly.

Once the chips are ready, carve the beef, season with good quality sea salt, serve with the salads and enjoy!

This is a next-level pork chop! Brining the meat the day before means it's really tender (though Newton Farm's pork doesn't need much help) and the herbs, garlic and sugar add a depth of flavour. The cider and mustard glaze is one of our favourites – mixed with local cream, it's the taste of Somerset in one delicious sauce. Whatever greens are in season are good with this – ideally kale or cavolo nero.

newton farm pork chop

Serves 4

For the brine

- 1 litre water
- 50g salt
- 50g soft dark brown sugar
- 1 sprig rosemary
- 3 sprigs thyme
- 4 garlic cloves, crushed
- 10 whole black peppercorns

For the pork

- 4 Newton Farm pork chops
- 1 tablespoon rapeseed oil
- 50g butter
- 4 garlic cloves, crushed
- 2 sprigs thyme
- 2 sprigs rosemary

For the cider and mustard sauce

- 150ml medium dry cider
- 500ml beef stock
- 1 teaspoon cider brandy (we get ours from the Somerset Cider Brandy Company)
- 80-90ml double cream
- 1 tablespoon wholegrain mustard

For the veg

- 400g bunch of kale or cavolo nero
- knob of butter
- salt and pepper

The day before you plan to serve, make the brine by heating all the ingredients together until the sugar is dissolved – keep stirring it so that the sugar doesn't stick to the bottom. Once the sugar has dissolved, leave the brine to cool at room temperature. When it's fully cooled, submerge the chops and leave for 12 hours in the fridge. When ready to cook, wash off and pat dry with a kitchen towel.

For the cider and mustard sauce, put the cider in a pan and reduce to 1 tablespoon thick glaze (this will take a good 5 minutes, but keep an eye on it – once it starts getting syrupy it can burn quickly). Set to one side.

Reduce the beef stock by two-thirds to intensify the flavour and thicken up. Add the cider reduction and the cider brandy to the beef stock and cook for about 1 minute. Add the cream and bring to a gentle boil; stir in the mustard then remove from the heat.

Heat the oven to 220°C, 200°C fan (425°F), Gas Mark 7.

To cook the chops, heat the rapeseed oil in a ribbed griddle pan and seal them on medium to high heat. Rotate them after 2 minutes to get a nice criss-cross pattern then repeat this on the other side. Now sear the fat along the edge for a couple of minutes to crisp up and colour. Put the chops on a baking tray and top with the butter, garlic and herbs. Roast in the oven for 6 minutes then rest for 5.

Meanwhile, prep the kale or cavolo nero by stripping the leaves from the stalks. Blanch the leaves in a pan of boiling water for 1-2 minutes (depending on how soft you like your greens). Drain and place in a pan with a knob of butter and season with salt and pepper. Toss and serve with the pork chops and the cider and mustard sauce.

CIDER WITH SOPHIE

Somerset is cider country, and bar manager Sophie makes sure there's always a scrumptious range on offer, a world away from the mass-produced stuff of our 1970s and 1980s youths. 'We're spoilt for choice for cider here,' says Sophie. 'Somerset and cider have a long, romantic history. Brought to the country by the Romans, there are records of cider production here since the 11th century, and it was often used as payment for a hard day's labour in the fields.' In addition to well-known makers such as Thatcher's and Sheppy's, there are small, family-run businesses like Chew Valley Blackbird and Pilton Cider doing great things. Then, as Sophie explains, 'there are exciting producers like Pulpt, who produce "new-fashioned cider" and Iford – completely bonkers stuff! Somerset is to cider what Bordeaux is to wine, and I love that it's all made down the road.'

04

NATURALISTS AND NATURISTS

DORSET

ON THE BEACH

Ferry Slipway 150 yds

BEACH

South Beach
COAST PATH 3
StHavenPoint

1636

Robin: We searched long and hard for a seaside hotel in an unspoilt rural setting, driving the south coast from Brighton to Bournemouth. I came to realise that as a nation we've done a pretty good job of messing up our coastline – turning it into one long conurbation of uninspiring and uncoordinated buildings. So I decided to broaden the search westward, and chartered a boat and skipper to motor up the coastline from Weymouth to Poole, to see if there was anything visible from the water. It was from the boat that I first saw the Manor House Hotel in Studland, occupying what I think is probably the finest unspoilt site on the south coast within easy striking distance of London – largely thanks to the work of the National Trust. Fortunately for us, the owners were happy to sell. And what an extraordinary building it is – part fantasy castle, part gingerbread house – from day one The Pig-on the Beach has captured the imagination of our guests. The most common complaint is, 'I love it, but I can never get in!' All I'd say is, keep trying!

THERE'S SOMETHING ABOUT THIS CRAZY OLD GINGERBREAD HOUSE LOOKING OUT TO OLD HARRY ROCKS THAT PUTS A SMILE ON EVERYONE'S FACE. IT'S EITHER THAT OR THE NUDISTS IN THE DUNES

There's something about The Pig-on the Beach that makes everyone smile. Maybe it's the sight of this crazy old gingerbread house perched up on the cliff, looking out to Old Harry Rocks. Or maybe it's knowing that just down the way there's a load of naturists in the sand dunes. Whatever it is, this is a happy place. There's something deeply English about it, with a hint of the Famous Five – Enid Blyton did holiday in Studland, after all. One of the things we love about this spot is its beach-hutted, sandy-toed charm. Although Studland is part of the mainland, this area is called the Isle of Purbeck and it's true it has an island vibe – it's probably that ferry ride from Poole that does it.

The house itself is an eccentric gem, built as a seaside bolthole by George Henry Bankes, MP in 1825 for his wife and their 14 children. George spent his retirement enlarging and improving the house, hence its higgledy-piggledy appeal. The family were descendants of 'Brave Dame Mary' Bankes who defended Corfe Castle, up the road, from Cromwell's troops. Some of the medieval carvings in the house are said to have come from there. Some others, now in one of the bedrooms, were, shall we say, 'rescued' by George from the Palace of Westminster after the fire of 1834.

This part of Dorset is another hotbed of brilliant, independent farmers, fishermen and producers doing their own thing, reinventing old methods and trying new ideas. We feel very lucky to be part of it all. The kitchen gets to cook with the most amazing fresh fish, often delivered within an hour of landing, all through the year, and there are some of the country's most talented organic farmers on our doorstep. Plus, we've got the Jurassic Coast – and fossil heaven – nearby, a bit of top-notch wartime history (King George VI, Churchill, Eisenhower, Mountbatten and Montgomery watched a dummy run of the D-Day landings pretty much from our doorstep), one of the country's most special pubs, the Square & Compass in Worth Matravers, and the kiss-me-quick allure of Swanage. I mean, what more could you want?

MUSTO
EIGENDOM 2016

'I BOUGHT A LITTLE BOAT, GOT A FEW NETS AND STARTED LEARNING'

Ian 'Bert' Galbraith, COVE ON THE QUAY

A few times a week, Ian Galbraith, or Bert to us, turns up at the kitchen door with his haul, all of it as fresh as it gets. 'James or Andy (our head chef and area head chef here) will just give me a call and say, "We need 40 fish tonight."' Bert wasn't always a fisherman – he ran a pub on the quay at Poole. 'Then about 13 years ago, I got to know a few of the old fishermen down there and started going out fishing with them. I really liked it, so I bought a little boat, got a few nets and started learning.' From a small start with just one boat, the Macey Louis, Bert has expanded dramatically, especially during the pandemic, when people were looking for new, local sources of produce. He now has two more boats – Stella Amy and Goa Baby – and crew to help him, plus he buys from five or six other local fishermen in Poole and Weymouth, and runs the fish stall on Poole Quay with the help of his partner, Amy. The catch changes with the months: 'In early summer, we're fishing inshore because there's a lot of weed about so we don't want to go out to deeper waters. So we fish for sea bass, mullet and mackerel in Studland Bay and Shell Bay. Then it's red mullet and plaice until September, Dover sole from August to May, skate and bass all year round, and cockles and clams, of course.'

But despite the demands of running his booming business, Bert still goes out to fish himself whenever he can: 'I love it. I work all day handling the admin, then go out in the evening if I can. The harbour's beautiful at night: it's cool and no one's about. We go round the edge of Studland, over to the Old Harry Rocks, searching for shoals, then when we find them, put the nets down. My skill as a fisherman is growing all the time. I can pinpoint pretty much where there's going to be fish and when, knowing the weather and the tides.' But sometimes things don't quite go to plan: 'We nearly sank last year, fishing off Dolphin Sands off the Isle of Wight. We were out for two days and had too much gear on the boat and too many nets out as we knew a storm was coming. We pushed our luck and had so much weight that we started to fill up with water.' Luckily for Bert – and us – he made it back safely. We look forward to him turning up at the kitchen door for many years to come.

The fish that Bert (aka Ian Galbraith of Cove on the Quay in Poole) brings us is so fresh and delicious that less is more when it comes to cooking – you don't want to add anything that's too overpowering. Sea bass has a delicate sweetness to it, which the fennel and lemon in this recipe set off nicely. If you buy one big fish, it works well as a sharing plate, served with a zingy summer veg salad.

sea bass to share

For a sharing plate for 2–4

- 1 x 1-2kg sea bass (1kg fish serves 2)
- 1 lemon
- 1 bulb fennel (save the fronds for the salad)
- salt and pepper
- 200g butter, cut into pieces
- 250ml dry white wine

For the garden summer veg salad

- 80g fresh peas
- 60g sugar snap peas
- 4 radishes
- 2 sprigs flat leaf parsley, leaves only
- 8 young celery leaves
- fennel fronds (from the bulb)
- juice of 1 lemon (you'll need 40ml)
- 60ml rapeseed oil
- salt and pepper

Ask the fishmonger to scale and gut your fish.

Heat the oven to 200°C, 180°C fan (400°F), Gas Mark 6. Thinly slice the lemon and fennel and stuff inside the fish. Season the fish inside and out, put it on a large tray with the butter and wine and cook in the oven for 20-25 minutes (if you're using a smaller fish, look at it after 18 minutes). Check the flesh is firm and white. Spoon the juices over the top of the fish and rest for 10-15 minutes.

Pod the fresh peas. Finely slice the sugar snaps and radishes. Pick the parsley and celery leaves and roughly shred. Chop the fennel fronds. Dress the vegetables with the lemon juice and oil and lightly season. Add the herbs just before serving.

Put the fish on a plate along with the cooked fennel and a generous helping of the vibrant salad. For a more hearty dinner, add chips!

'I TAKE THE CHEFS WHATEVER'S IN MY GARDEN AND THEY GIVE ME LOVELY DINNERS IN EXCHANGE'

Rachel Helfer, GARDENER, KNITSON OLD FARMHOUSE

Most of the people who supply our kitchens are pretty amazing, full of knowledge and passion for what they do, but Rachel Helfer has to be one of the most extraordinary. Rachel, who at the age of 87 still tends h beautiful, rambling Purbeck garden seven days a week is known to The Pig-on the Beach kitchen as 'the Kiwi Lady', because she has a huge, abundant kiwi tree that keeps our kitchen very happy in late summer. 'I call it triffid, because it's grown so big. Last year I put 500 ki aside for The Pig, quite small but with a lovely taste.' But here's the thing: no money changes hands. 'I have no idea of the price of anything, I don't buy anything (she is largely self-sufficient), so I give them whatever think they might like, and I get lovely meals in exchan They're always giving me dinners, it rather embarrasse me!' she says. The whole thing started because Rachel' daughter Rebecca and French son-in-law, Bruno, were big foragers, and came up with the idea of bartering th fungi with Andy, The Pig-on the Beach's original chef. Now she offers up not just kiwis, but whatever she has a glut of in her glorious sunny garden, where bantams potter among the poppies and apple trees.

A true original, Rachel has tended her organic garc here since 1952, when she moved from her parents' small dairy farm in Swanage. In 1956 she married her American husband, Mark, and went on to have five children (Mark sadly died 11 years ago): 'I always tried to grow enough food for the family because we never had any money, so the garden was laid out to feed a large family. Now the pressure is off, so I can grow wha I like – I have 20 different fruits: grapes, nashi pears, plums, greengages, apples, lemons, nut trees…' She imparts her wisdom with precision and a twinkle in he eye, throwing out pearls on everything from how to ea lemons (you have to eat the whole thing, including the rind, grated) to why apple pies should include quince. Other stories cover her love of skinny-dipping, her trailblazer grandmother, memories of giving riding lessons to a teenage Mia Farrow, and the importance o still riding her horse as she heads for 90. But it is her garden that keeps her going above everything: 'It is my great joy. When the Jehovah's Witnesses come calling I always tell them I have a Garden of Eden already; I do not need their prayers. We have a cup of coffee and a wonderful talk and they go on their way.'

Another dish that makes the most of our garden produce and keeps the plant-eaters happy! The lovely smoky taste of the charred peppers goes really well with the zesty quinoa and can be eaten hot or cold. During summer we're often left with a glut of chillies – our harissa dressing is a great way to preserve them. We keep it in the fridge and use it whenever we think something needs a bit of spicing up. If you prefer a milder heat, reduce the number of chillies.

stuffed romano peppers

Serves 4 as a main

- 8 Romano peppers (if we run out of our own, we use the fantastic sweet ones from the Isle of Wight)
- 1 medium onion, finely chopped
- a little rapeseed oil
- 200g Hodmedod's smoked quinoa (if you can't get this, red or white quinoa works fine)
- 500ml vegetable stock
- 2 tablespoons chopped parsley
- zest and juice of 1 lemon
- salt and pepper

For the harissa dressing

- 4 fresh red chillies
- 1 red pepper
- ½ teaspoon coriander seeds
- ¼ teaspoon cumin seeds
- ¼ teaspoon fennel seeds
- 1 garlic clove, crushed
- ½ teaspoon sea salt
- 1 teaspoon tomato purée
- 2 teaspoons lemon juice
- 4 drops rosewater
- 40g Dijon mustard
- 60ml white wine vinegar
- 1 teaspoon sugar
- 240ml rapeseed oil
- 20g water

First make the harissa dressing. Set the grill on high and place the chillies and red pepper on a tray. Grill until blistered and the skin is slightly blackened (they may pop so be careful when you take them from under the grill). Remove the stalks but leave the seeds in. Toast the coriander, cumin and fennel seeds in a dry frying pan until lightly coloured.

Place all the dressing ingredients in a food processor and blend together until smooth.

Blister the Romano peppers on the barbecue for 6-8 minutes (or in the oven on a wire rack at the highest temperature for 8-10 minutes). Sweat the onion in a little rapeseed oil.

Add the quinoa and stock and cook until the quinoa is tender, stirring often to prevent it sticking (this will take about 10 minutes). Finish with chopped parsley, lemon zest and juice, and salt and pepper to taste.

To serve, cut the peppers in half lengthways, remove the seeds, spoon over the quinoa and drizzle with the harissa dressing.

The word taffety comes from taffeta, as in the silk fabric used in ballgowns, but how it became associated with apple tart is anyone's guess! There are many variations of this pudding, mostly dating from Victorian times, but they all contain apple, with the addition of orange, rose, rhubarb, or – group pastry chef Kelvin's favourite – lemon. We think it's best served warm, along with a good old dousing of best Dorset cream.

taffety tart (aka dorset apple & lemon tart)

Serves 12

(You'll need a 23cm loose-bottomed tart case or flan ring)

For the pastry

- 175g plain flour
- 20g icing sugar
- pinch of salt
- 50g semolina
- zest and juice of 1 large lemon
- 115g unsalted butter

For the filling

- 3-4 large Bramley apples
- zest and juice of 1 lemon
- 3 large eggs plus 2 yolks
- 175g caster sugar

Sieve the flour, sugar and salt into a mixing bowl, then add the semolina.

Gently heat the lemon zest, juice and butter until just bubbling, then remove from the heat and leave to cool for a few minutes. Gradually add the buttery mix to the flour mix and bind together to make a dough. This is a slightly crumbly pastry, so be careful not to overmix it.

Wrap or cover the pastry and leave to rest in the fridge for 30 minutes (it'll set too firm if you chill it for much longer).

On a lightly floured surface, roll out the dough and line your tart case or flan ring. Chill for at least 30 minutes.

Heat the oven to 180°C, 160°C fan (350°F), Gas Mark 4. Remove the pastry case from the fridge and line with greaseproof paper or clingfilm. Fill with baking beans, rice or flour, gently pushing the filling into the corners to stop the pastry from collapsing. Place on the middle shelf for 12-16 minutes, then carefully remove the filling and paper.

Using a fork, gently prick the pastry base and return to the oven for a further 12-16 minutes or until it's dry and slightly coloured. Now remove it from the oven and glaze with leftover egg white to seal up any holes. Leave to cool at room temperature.

Peel, core and finely grate the Bramleys (you want to end up with 450g grated flesh). Add the lemon zest and juice to the apple straight away to stop it from browning.

In a mixing bowl, beat together the whole eggs, yolks and sugar, add the apple and mix well. Pour into the cooled pastry case and return to the oven for 35-40 minutes – the top should be golden, and check that the centre is just cooked with a cocktail stick.

This can be served cold, but it's better warm (though not hot as it won't cut well!), with pouring cream, ice cream or custard.

4PM: HOUSEKEEPING

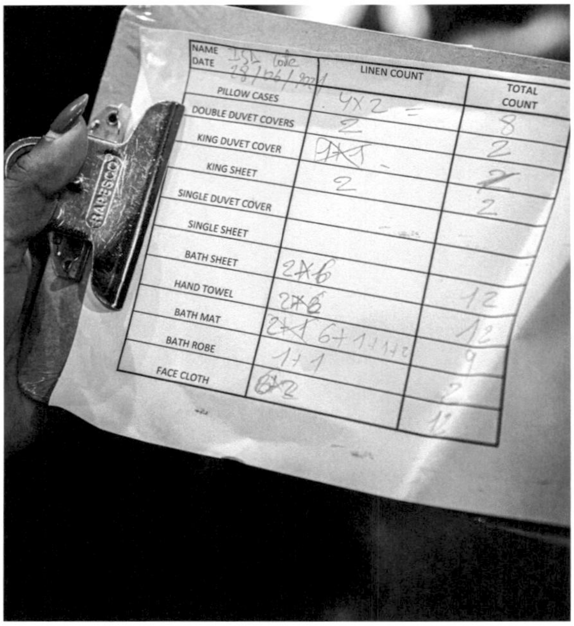

'IT'S A CASE OF LOOK AFTER THE SOIL AND THE SOIL WILL LOOK AFTER YOU'

Andrew and Claire Head, CEDAR ORGANIC

Andrew Head is one of the country's most dedicated farmers, and his methods are second to none. He spent 13 years helping to shape Carole Bamford's Daylesford and Wootton estates into the benchmark for organic farming before moving with his wife, Claire, to set up Cedar Organic at the picturesque Rempstone Farm in the heart of the Isle of Purbeck, just down the road from The Pig-on The Beach. The way they describe their approach makes it sound simple: look after the soil and the soil will look after you. 'Regenerative agriculture has become a buzzword lately,' says Andrew. 'We've been doing it here for 15 years. It's organic farming in its truest sense; allowing the natural processes to take place, rebuilding soil health. The soil food web is what does the hard work for us.'

Of course, it's not entirely a case of leaving the land to its own devices. In recent years, Andrew has started planting herbal leys – a hardy mix of grasses, herbs and legumes – that have not only left their pastures 'luxuriating in moisture', but their cattle, sheep and chickens in particularly rude health.

'We're grazing them on chicory, plantain, cocksfoot, red clover and sheep's parsley; forage with long roots that draw nutrients and minerals from deep in the ground. It improves the health of the animals no end.' This kind of animal husbandry allows them to keep their stock considerably longer than most. They rear their North Devon Ruby Red beef calves for over three years (cattle are usually finished in less than 30 months) and as well as selling us succulent lamb, they also sell hogget.

'Hogget has the most tremendous flavour,' says Andrew. 'Fast-grown spring lamb has a more delicate flavour, while hogget is the ultimate slow-grown lamb. It's grown for a full year, unbred, and with a much broader diet. We graze our sheep – New Zealand Romney – in a range of habitats, from the chalk grasslands of the Purbeck Ridge down through the heathland to the drier sandy grounds and fertile fields. The sheep are happier, healthier, fatter and tastier for it. It's a bit like salt marsh lamb."

Curiously, hogget still gets treated like mutton, so farmers are generally offered half the price of lamb if they sell to supermarkets or wholesale. Fortunately, Andrew prefers to sell locally and our head chef James can't get enough of it. We think it's worth every penny.

Lots of people, when they see hogget on the menu, think it's something to do with pigs. But it's actually the word for a lamb in its second spring or summer, so aged between one and two. Ours come from Cedar Organic, a farm with some of the best animal husbandry methods we've come across (not to mention spectacular views over Studland). The extra months on pasture mean the flavour is deeper and fuller than lamb's, but the meat is still really tender. This is a great Sunday lunch sharing dish and can be served on a platter with roasted baby carrots, boiled new potatoes or whatever your family's go-to veg are. The carrot top green sauce adds a zesty kick.

roast hogget leg, carrot top green sauce

Serves 6–8

- 2kg hogget leg (or lamb)
- 3 litres whey
- 150g salt
- 4 garlic cloves
- 4 rosemary sprigs

For an alternative brine

- 2.5 litres water
- 125g salt
- 2 bay leaves
- 6 peppercorns
- 2 sprigs rosemary
- 2 garlic cloves
- 2 allspice berries

For the carrot top green sauce

- 2 banana shallots
- 1 garlic clove
- zest and juice of 1 lemon
- 3 tablespoons lilliput capers, roughly chopped
- salt and pepper
- 8 tablespoons rapeseed oil
- 2 handfuls carrot tops, finely chopped
- 1 bunch mint, finely chopped

Ask the butcher to bone out the leg, leaving the shinbone in place, and roll it. If you can't get hogget, lamb will work.

Warm a little of the whey, dissolve the salt in it and return to the rest. Whey isn't the easiest to get hold of, so you can make the alternative brine instead. For the non-whey brine, bring everything to the boil, turn off the heat and leave to cool.

Submerge the leg into whichever brine you're using; leave overnight.

When you're ready to cook, heat the oven to 200°C, 180°C fan (400°F), Gas Mark 6. Take the lamb from the brine and pat dry. Stud it with the garlic and rosemary and roast in the oven for 1hr 15 minutes. Rest for at least 30 minutes before carving. Enjoy with your favourite roast accompaniments and the green sauce.

For the green sauce, finely dice the shallots and mince the garlic. Add lemon zest and juice, capers, a pinch of salt and pepper and the oil. Just before serving, stir through the carrot tops and mint.

Blackberries are one of the compensations for the end of summer, and our hedgerows here in Dorset are filled with really juicy, sweet ones. This recipe pairs an old-fashioned creamy syllabub with the berries, which provide just the right amount of fruity zing. Save the prettiest berries for the final flourish.

dorset lavender syllabub with hedgerow blackberries

Serves 4

- zest and juice of 1 lemon (you'll need 40ml)
- 2 sprigs lavender, well bruised
- 90ml sparkling wine (we use the fantastic Langham Classic Cuvée from Dorset)
- 30ml brandy
- 80g honey (we use the honey from our hives)
- 300ml double cream
- 24 blackberries
- 1 teaspoon caster sugar

In a jar, place the lemon zest, juice, lavender and alcohol. Cover with a lid or clingfilm and leave overnight.

The next day, pass the liquid through a fine sieve into a pan and heat gently. Add the honey and stir to melt; leave to cool.

Whisk the cream until it starts to thicken, then slowly add the cooled alcohol while still whisking (it'll thicken to a soft whip). Pour into 4 suitable glasses and chill.

Wash the blackberries and put aside the best half.

Place the remainder in a pan, sprinkle with the sugar and a dash of water, then gently heat just enough to break down the berries. Remove from the heat and allow to cool to room temperature.

Remove the chilled syllabub from the fridge and top with the cooked berries and any juices, then add the fresh berries.

Even people who love their fish often don't know about Arctic char. It's delicate in flavour, a bit like sea trout, but similar to sea bass in texture. It belongs to the salmon and trout family (but less fatty, so very healthy) and is normally only found in the freezing waters around the Arctic Circle – except if you live in Dorset! That's because up the road at Houghton Springs Fish Farm there's an aquaculture boffin called Hans Hoff who's magicked Arctic char into the Stour, the beautiful chalk stream near Blandford Forum. We serve it in thick steaks with lashings of hollandaise.

arctic char

Serves 4

- 2 bunches asparagus
- 1 Arctic char weighing 1kg, cut into 4 steaks across the bone (trout is the closest alternative)
- a little rapeseed oil
- 1 lemon, cut into 4 wedges

For the hollandaise

- 250g butter
- 1 egg yolk
- ½ teaspoon tarragon vinegar
- salt and pepper
- a splash of lemon juice

Prep the asparagus by snapping off the bottom woody part of the spear. Bring a pan of salted water to the boil, add the asparagus and simmer until just cooked, leaving a little bite.

To make the hollandaise, melt the butter until the fat and milk have separated. Whisk the egg yolk with the vinegar in a bowl over a pan of gently simmering water until the yolk has thickened. Slowly pour the melted butter into the bowl, whisking continuously so it doesn't split. Stop once all the butterfat is used and you're left with just the white buttermilk. Discard this. Season the hollandaise and add a splash of lemon juice. Keep it warm.

Heat the oven to 200°C, 180°C fan (400°F), Gas Mark 6. Season the fish with salt and pepper then sear for about 1 minute in a hot griddle pan with a little oil. Flip over with a fish slice (so that both sides have griddle marks) and fry for another minute. Put on a foil-lined baking tray and cook in the oven for 6-8 minutes. Leave to rest. The flesh should just start to come away from the bone.

Divide the asparagus between plates, place the char on top and serve the hollandaise either over the fish or on the side, with a wedge of lemon.

We've had this on the menu since the opening of The Pig-on the Beach. It's a play on a classic that uses mussels, but is a perfect way to showcase the amazing cockles and clams we have here in Dorset. So easy to make, even after a glass or three of rosé. We like to cook it in our outdoor pizza oven, but any stove or hob will do.

wood-roasted dorset cockles & clams

Serves 2

- 500g clams
- 500g cockles
- 1 tablespoon rapeseed oil
- 2 banana shallots, finely chopped
- 6 sprigs thyme
- 75ml dry white wine
- salt and pepper
- 75ml double cream
- 1 tablespoon chopped parsley
- juice of 1 lemon

Rinse the clams and cockles in cold water then soak them in fresh water for 30 minutes to flush out any sand and silt. Discard any that are open or have chips out of the shell, then rinse again.

With your pizza oven already hot, place a heavy-bottomed pan inside. Alternatively, put your pan on the hob at a medium to high heat and follow the same method below.

Add the oil and fry the shallots and thyme until soft. Add the clams, cockles, wine and some salt and pepper.

Cover with a lid and steam until all the shellfish have opened – this will take about 3-4 minutes; discard any that stay closed.

Add the cream, parsley and lemon juice. Taste and correct seasoning before serving with some lovely fresh sourdough.

STUDLAND TO BROCKENHURST - 44 MILES

05

FROM LITTLE ACORNS TO MIGHTY OAKS

HAMPSHIRE

IN THE FOREST

NEW FOREST
NATIONAL PARK

Havana
Cigars
Available
Here.

Robin: Well, this is where it all started back in 2011. Deep in the ancient New Forest near Brockenhurst sat Whitley Ridge Hotel. The eureka moment was seeing its perfectly formed kitchen garden with only weeds and a couple of carrots in residence. It all seems perfectly obvious now... the idea of creating a relaxed, homely, unstuffy country-house hotel with the focus on homegrown produce from a kitchen garden that would inform everything from the menu to the interior design. The stable yard offered the opportunity to expand the bedroom count to a viable number, and we converted the lakeside shelter to our first Potting Shed treatment hut. When the doors were thrown open to The Pig in July 2011, no one, least of all us, believed that 10 years later we would have a collection of Pig hotels across nearly every county in the south of England. They've certainly been fun times.

IN THESE ANCIENT WOODS WITH THEIR WILD PONIES AND OLD STONE LODGES, IT'S ALL CRACKLING FIRES, DEEP COMFORTS AND MOREISH FLAVOURS

There are special places, and then there are unique places. The New Forest is unlike anywhere else in Britain, and as the home of our very first Pig, it couldn't be closer to our hearts. It's hard to believe, when you turn off the motorway past Southampton, how quickly you enter another world: an ancient landscape of sandy heathland, wild ponies, deep forest and rich pasture, all giving way to little harbours and creeks looking out onto the Solent and across to the Isle of Wight. We opened our original Pig here at Brockenhurst in 2011, and although each hotel is very much itself, so much of what we do started here: the walled garden, the huts, the 25-mile menus, the Potting Shed treatment rooms, the open fires, upcycled furniture, the animals. Even the coloured glasses in the windows came about because the bar at Brockenhurst didn't have space for a separate glass cupboard, so someone had the bright idea of putting glass shelves into the window casement.

The original house here was built in 1602 as a groomkeeper's lodge – the New Forest was created in the 11th century (not so new then) as a hunting ground for William the Conqueror, and by the 17th century was divided into bailiwicks, each with its own lodge. We love ours and, amid these ancient woods, it's a place of deep comfort and moreish flavours – all misty mornings, wood-smoke evenings, pigs snuffling for acorns and the earthy flavours of mushroom, wood pigeon and deer. We also have the fishermen of Dorset on our doorstep, and the farmers and makers of Wiltshire and Hampshire to inspire us, so our chefs really are spoilt for choice. And if you go down to the fields beyond the walled garden, you might just meet the original pig of the original Pig: a kunekune – he's not exactly a looker, but he's been with us from the start, and we love him.

THIS LITTLE PIGGY WENT TO PANNAGE

The New Forest is the only area of the country where the ancient custom of pannage – allowing pigs to roam free in the forest to feast on acorns and other nuts – still continues. It's one of six ancient rights that were granted to commoners in the time of William the Conqueror, and serves not only to fatten the pigs on the fruits of the forest, but to help protect the New Forest's ponies and cattle, as acorns can prove toxic to many animals. It makes for a fabulous sight in autumn: the pigs are allowed to roam the forest for two months from September (the exact date is dependent on when the acorns fall each year), but they have been known to go trotting off further afield, running along roads and turning up in local villages. We get our pannage pork from Sonja Waite, who raises British heritage breeds near Beaulieu, and it's superb quality, tender and full of forest flavour. It doesn't appear on our menu for long, and is incredibly popular, so make sure you book well ahead for pannage season!

Pannage is an extremely exciting time of year, not only because you get to see pigs roaming free in the forest but also because you know their incredible meat is soon to follow – so for a few precious weeks every autumn this dish is on our menu. The black garlic butter with oyster mushrooms grown in our mushroom house is one of our favourite pairings. We use black garlic from The Garlic Farm on the Isle of Wight, available in farm shops and online. We repurposed our old walk-in fridge for our mushroom house at The Pig, where we grow a range of fungi using recycled coffee grounds.

pannage pork, black garlic oyster mushrooms

Serves 2

For the pork

- 1 pannage pork tenderloin, weighing 400–500g
- 1 tablespoon vegetable oil
- 25g butter
- 3 garlic cloves, crushed
- 4 sprigs winter savoury

For the black garlic butter

- 125g salted butter at room temperature
- 25g black garlic, peeled
- zest of ½ lemon
- ½ banana shallot, finely diced
- 10g parsley, chopped

For the mushrooms and broccoli

- 1 tablespoon vegetable oil
- 100g oyster mushrooms (halve them if they're big)
- 100g purple-sprouting (or Tenderstem) broccoli (split it if it's large)
- 200ml red wine sauce (you can get good quality sauces from the chilled aisle in the supermarket)

Heat the oven to 220°C, 200°C fan (425°F), Gas Mark 7. Using a sharp knife, remove the sinew from the tenderloin – take care not to cut too deep and waste any of the meat. Season well with salt and pepper. Bring a frying pan up to a high heat. Add the oil and the tenderloin (you can cut the pork in half if that makes it more manageable); turn regularly until all the sides are golden brown. Add the butter, garlic and herbs and baste by spooning the oil over it. Cook in the oven for 4-5 minutes and rest for 3 minutes before serving. Your pork should be blushing.

Soften the salted butter. Place the black garlic into a mixing bowl and, using a fork or spoon, crush to a paste. Add the rest of the ingredients plus the butter and mix well. Spoon the butter onto a sheet of parchment paper. Make a sausage shape by rolling up the parchment then chill.

Place a frying pan on a high heat and add the vegetable oil. Add the mushrooms and cook until slightly softened and starting to turn golden. Add the broccoli and season with salt and pepper, then add 50g of the black garlic butter (the rest can go into the fridge or freezer for later, maybe for a risotto or any number of dishes). Cook until the broccoli is softened but still has some bite. Once the pork has rested, slice it into thick rounds and put on a plate with the broccoli and mushrooms. Finish with the red wine sauce, gently heated through.

7.30AM: KITCHEN GARDEN

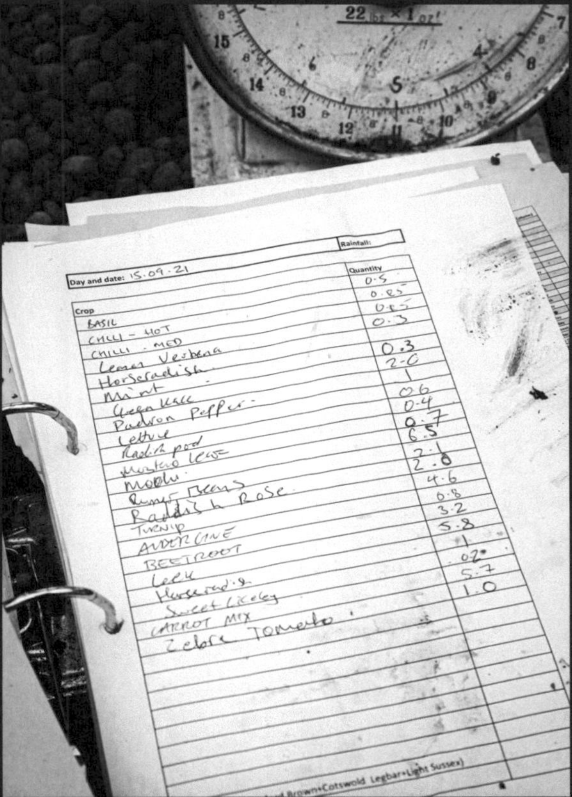

Rainfall:
Day and date: 15.09.21
Quantity
Crop
BASIL
CHILLI - HOT
CHILLI - MED
Lemon Verbena
Horseradish
Mint
Green Kale
Padron Pepper
Lettuce
Radish pod
Runner Beans
Radish Rose
Turnip
AUBERGINE
BEETROOT
Leek
Horseradish
Sweet Cicely
CARROT MIX
Zebra Tomato
0.5
0.3
2.0
0.6
0.4
0.7
6.5
4.6
0.8
3.2
5.8
5.7
1.0
Cotswold Legbar+Light Sussex)

OLLIE'S WEIRD & WONDERFUL FRUIT & VEG

One of the things that Ollie, our group head kitchen gardener, loves most is researching some of the more obscure or forgotten veg out there, and getting it going in our own kitchen gardens. Ollie uses lots of different seed suppliers and is often to be found spending his evenings trawling through specialist vegetable websites, searching for the next up-and-coming voguish veg to get our chefs excited about. Some of the new staples of our kitchen gardens are standard in another part of the world, but viewed as a rare delicacy here; other times it will be something that was once an everyday ingredient but has been forgotten. Over to Ollie...

1 Sea kale *Crambe maritima*

About 10 years ago I asked a forager friend to collect some sea kale seeds for me. They germinated very successfully and the sea kale in all our gardens has been propagated from those plants. You need to force sea kale in early spring by placing a pot over the dormant crowns, just as the small purple buds start to appear around March or early April. Once the tender forced shoots start to grow they can be harvested before they reach the top of their pots, at which point they have an earthy, sweet and nutty flavour. Sea kale is a great example of how our eating habits have changed: it was once known as poor man's asparagus in coastal communities, but now sells for high prices to top restaurants.

2 Agretti *Salsola soda*

Agretti is a fantastically succulent vegetable from the Mediterranean with a mildly salty, spinach-like taste. In Italy, it is known as *barba di frate*, which means monk's beard. In the UK, we tend to steam and butter it and treat it more as a green, whereas in Italy they eat it raw, serving it more as a salad, with olive oil, lemon juice and black pepper. We like to treat ours as a zero-miles alternative to samphire. The chefs steam or pickle it, and we often use it to garnish fish dishes. One tip: it's worth buying new seeds every year, as the germination of old seeds can be a bit erratic. This is because they're not true seeds, but leaf embryos.

3 Chilean guava *Ugni molinae*

We first started growing Chilean guava as a bit of an experiment back in 2013 when we began restoring the kitchen gardens at The Pig-near Bath. While not producing the fist-sized guavas that grow in the tropics, these hardy evergreen perennials produce hundreds of small fruits about the size of the tip of your little finger. They are harvested in late autumn, just when other fruits have finished, and have a fantastic smell and taste – a hint of wild strawberry and kiwi, but with some definite tropical notes. Introduced to the UK in 1844, they developed a reputation for being Queen Victoria's favourite fruit. I enjoy them mixed into a bowl of yoghurt with our honey.

4 Oyster Plant *Mertensia maritima*

Several years ago, a few of our kitchen gardeners and chefs visited Simon Rogan's gastro temple, L'Enclume in Cumbria, and while being shown around their garden we were blown away by the uncanny oyster-like flavour of these succulent blue-green-tinged leaves. As soon as we left, we sourced some so we could start growing it. A close relative of borage, oyster plant grows natively around the sub-Arctic coasts of northern Europe and goes by the common name 'sea bluebells'. We use it as a garnish on seafood dishes, although it can also be used as flavouring for vegan oysters.

5 Japanese wineberries *Rubus phoenicolasius*

I first became aware of the Japanese wineberry in Mark Diacono's excellent book A Taste of the Unexpected. This Asian cousin of our native raspberry and blackberry plants forms a thick forest of curved stems covered in tiny, red needle-like thorns. In late summer, the white flowers develop into small, reddy-orange clusters of hugely abundant berries that are similar in shape to some of the smaller blackberry varieties, but taste like raspberries. Propagation is via a natural process known as layering, whereby the plant stems fall over, producing roots at the point where the stems touch the ground. Our pastry chefs use these fruits in all kinds of dishes, but a favourite is set in a gin jelly.

PHOTOGRAPH OF JAPANESE WINEBERRY BY MARK DIACONO

1

2

3

4

5

José is our wood oven chef, and over the years we've all got to know how passionate he is about Spanish food. He even has a YouTube channel dedicated to teaching traditional Spanish recipes. We've made gazpacho for years, but this year (after watching one of our garnish chefs preparing our usual recipe) José couldn't contain himself and showed us how to make it his way, in traditional Andalusian style. It's truly delicious and encapsulates what we're forever striving for – simple, fresh food. Only one thing: José says we shouldn't call it soup, because then everyone thinks it's cooked. He calls it liquid salad. And it is!

josé's polytunnel gazpacho

Serves 4 (as a small starter)

- 500g tomatoes
- ½ cucumber, peeled
- 1 small green pepper, deseeded
- 100ml olive oil
- 2 garlic cloves, peeled
- 30g white bread, crusts removed
- 150ml water
- 1 teaspoon salt
- 2 tablespoons sherry vinegar

Roughly chop your tomatoes, cucumber and pepper. Put everything apart from the salt and vinegar into a blender and whizz for 4 minutes on a high speed until smooth. Pass through a fine sieve then add the salt and vinegar. Taste and add more if you need to.

We get a bumper harvest of onions every year. This dish really showcases their flavour and versatility, and can be served as a side or the main event for a light lunch. By burning the onions, you start to draw out a hint of bitterness that perfectly complements their sweetness and the acidity of the walnut ketchup.

garden onions, pickled walnut ketchup

Serves 4 as a starter

For the onions

- 8 small to medium onions (or 16 baby onions)
- 2 tablespoons vegetable oil
- 50g butter
- 6 garlic cloves, crushed
- 8 sprigs thyme
- 4 sprigs rosemary
- 500ml vegetable stock

For the pickled walnut ketchup

- 1 x 390g jar Opies Pickled Walnuts, including a quarter of the brine
- 1 tablespoon Dijon mustard
- 150ml vegetable oil

To finish

- 2 tablespoons fruit vinegar (we use Wild Island raspberry vinegar, available online)
- 4 tablespoons olive (or cold pressed rapeseed) oil
- handful of watercress

Heat your oven to 200°C, 180°C fan (400°F), Gas Mark 6. Peel and halve the onions. Place a large thick-based frying pan over a high heat until hot. Add the vegetable oil and onions, cut side down. Cook until well coloured (resist the temptation to move them around). When they're golden brown (and black in places), turn them over and add the butter, garlic, herbs, salt and pepper. Cook for a few minutes more to colour and soften further.

Pour your vegetable stock into a deep baking dish. Add the onions with the butter, garlic and herbs. Bake in the oven for 15-20 minutes. Test with a bluntish knife to check that the onions are cooked.

For the ketchup, place the walnuts, mustard and oil into a blender or food processor and whizz until smooth. Season with salt and pepper to taste. This makes more than you need, but it'll keep in the fridge for two weeks and can be used with other dishes.

Now combine the vinegar and oil, and dress the watercress. Spread the ketchup on your plate. Add the onions and watercress. And why not add a few toasted seeds for a bit of crunch? The leftover cooking juices are delicious and can be used as a base for a Sunday roast gravy.

'I'M A REFORMED VEGAN. IF ONLY MY 20-YEAR-OLD SELF COULD SEE ME NOW!'

Ericka Golding & Lee Moreton, FROM SALT TO SMOKE

'I'm a reformed vegan,' admits Ericka Golding, founder of the butcher From Salt to Smoke in Cranborne, Dorset, which supplies us with some of our more unusual cuts of meat. 'I laugh to myself sometimes when I walk into the fridge and see carcasses hanging everywhere. If only my 20-year-old self could see me now ...'

Ericka, who used to work for us, is married to James, our meat-loving chef director so, to be honest, we're pretty surprised she managed to stick to the veg for so long. However, it was the work of the revered ecologist Allan Savory that convinced her that cultivating livestock could be a force for good – even more so than the hearty aromas wafting from the family kitchen.

From Salt to Smoke was conceived during lockdown in response to friends saying they were finding it hard to track down really great meat. This got Ericka thinking: could she connect ethical and sustainable farmers with the most creative butchers and the most demanding restaurants?

'We're the middleman between the farmer and the restaurant,' explains Lee Moreton, one of two expert butchers Ericka recruited. 'The Pig does a lot of in-house butchery, but they often call on us for whole animals. We can source them, hang them, and then butcher them to really particular specifications.'

Lee practises what is known as 'seam butchery', a more skilful approach to meat portioning that focuses on individual muscles as opposed to larger joints. The benefits are manifold. When you roast a leg of lamb, for example, the shank takes longer to cook, which means the rump and centre cut can often be slightly overdone. Cooking individual muscles is far more focused in this respect. Plus, seam butchery is where the concept of nose-to-tail was established – not even an ounce of fat goes to waste.

'For The Pig, we would seam out the forequarter – a cut that would traditionally be used for stewing – and we'd get feather steaks and top blades that are perfect for salads,' explains Lee. 'By putting the time into the butchery and removing the sinew, you get a really tender, marbled piece of meat that takes a fraction of the time to cook.'

Their lamb often comes from the same flock of ewe that provides the milk for The Book & Bucket Cheese Company, based right next door. Beef mostly comes from the Cranborne Estate, grazed in the local water meadow. And then there's the charcuterie… Lee says it's all down to curing the meat with Himalayan salt. We reckon there must be more to it than that, but he's keeping schtum.

BLOOD
SWEAT
AND
GEARS
BRAKEBURN

Pannage Coppa
Pannage Ham
Air Dried Fallow
Chorizo Lomo
Mutton Ham

It's almost worrying how much cheese we
The Pig, and that amount has only skyrock
cheesemaker Peter Morgan paid us a visit a
Beach just over two years ago. Peter had re
Book & Bucket Cheese Company, not far a
of Cranborne and, much to our delight, he
some of his Hardy's (a hard cheese similar
Hemingway (a feta matured in Kalamata o
a revelation. We immediately placed a who
little did we know at the time – became his

'I started making cheese in a 20-litre ba
Peter, who has since won countless awards
'It's very much a bucket science, as they sa
something you like, you move to a bigger b
now operating out of two 500-litre cheese
appealed to us about Peter's cheese, other
course, is just how ultra-local the entire op
sheep's milk comes from ewes at the farm
made into cheese within 24 hours of milkin
Wilde – all of Peter's cheeses are named af
is foraged from the Cranborne Estate, and
comes from a producer down the road. We
so much we even held a competition for ou
soft cheese that he'd made especially for u
later, (Beatrix) Potter emerged as the winn
the key ingredient in our cheesecakes.

Our chef director James worked with P
cheese especially for The Pig, called Goldin
but happily also that of the great writer Wi
James was keen to develop a pressed ricott
always loved, but in the process Peter came
that far surpasses the initial idea. 'The add
sea salt produced some surprising results,'
also added some locally sourced black truf
take it to another level.'

'IT'S VERY MUCH A BUCKET SCIENCE. WHEN YOU FIND SOMETHING YOU LIKE, YOU MOVE TO A BIGGER BUCKET'

Peter Morgan, BOOK & BUCKET

This is a classic dish that again is all about simplicity, allowing the ingredients to do the talking. We know it's not for everyone – many people have stories of ordering this in a restaurant without realising it's served raw! We source our beef fillet from our friends at From Salt to Smoke, who salt-age the beef for us for up to 60 days, which gives it an incredible depth of flavour. When you're making this at home, get the freshest, highest-quality aged beef you can, from a local butcher rather than a supermarket.

beef tartare

Serves 4 as a small starter

For the tartare mix

- 150g salt-aged beef fillet, finely diced
- 15g lilliput capers (or chopped capers)
- 15g gherkins, finely diced
- 15g shallot, finely diced
- 2 teaspoons chopped parsley
- 1 tablespoon tomato ketchup
- 1 teaspoon Dijon mustard
- ½ teaspoon Worcestershire sauce
- a few drops of Tabasco, depending on how spicy you like it
- 4 egg yolks – as fresh as possible! Quail's eggs are good as they're smaller

For the croutons

- 4 thin slices sourdough (it can be a little stale)
- olive oil
- a pinch of chopped rosemary
- a pinch of chopped thyme
- sea salt flakes

Heat the oven to 180°C, 160°C fan (350°F), Gas Mark 4. Put your sourdough slices onto a baking tray and drizzle a little olive oil over the top. Sprinkle over the rosemary, thyme and salt flakes. Bake for 15 minutes or till toasted and golden.

Take a sharp knife and chopping board and dice the beef as small as you can. Combine all the wet and dry components apart from the yolks and season to taste with salt and pepper.

When you serve this, you can either use a metal ring or spoon it straight onto the plate. It's best served at room temperature to give maximum flavour. Finish by making a small well in the meat and place your yolk in the middle. Season it with a little salt and serve with the croutons.

This feels like pure New Forest to us – we're lucky to have lots of wood pigeon locally, but wherever you live, you should be able to buy it from a good butcher. It's really versatile and can be served as a starter or easily doubled up as a sharing dish. To get the best flavour, and keep the meat tender, pigeon is ideally served medium rare, but if this isn't how you like it, just cook the meat for an extra minute each side. The lightness of the vegetables helps to balance the richness of the pigeon breast – delicious!

wood pigeon & vegetables

Makes 4

For the vegetables

- 150g diced carrots – around the size of the broad beans
- 75g butter
- 100ml vegetable stock
- 150g peas
- 150g broad beans
- 150g chopped asparagus
- pinch of chopped mint
- pinch of chopped parsley

For the pigeon

- 4 pigeon breasts
- 2 tablespoons vegetable oil
- 50g butter
- 4 garlic cloves, crushed
- 6 sprigs thyme

Start with the vegetables. Bring a small pan of water to the boil and season with a little salt. Add the carrots, boil for 1 minute, remove and put into cold water. Melt the butter in a frying pan over a medium heat; once it's foaming, slowly add the stock, keeping the pan moving all the time to bring the butter and stock together. Add all the vegetables and warm through, stirring continuously. Finish with the herbs and season to taste.

Place a frying pan on a high heat. Season both sides of the pigeon with salt and pepper. Add the oil to the hot pan, then the pigeon, turning every 30 seconds for 4-5 minutes (depending on the size). Add the butter, garlic and thyme, remove from the heat and baste the pigeon breasts. Rest for 1 minute, then serve with the vegetables.

10PM: DINNER SERVICE

This is cheesecake but not as you know it. The honey adds a lovely sweetness to the base and the Potter soft cheese from Book & Bucket makes it extra special. We ran a competition for The Pig guests to name one of our favourite local maker's new cheeses, and the winner by a mile was Potter, of Peter Rabbit fame. It's beautifully creamy, which works well with that zesty dash of lemon. We grow a few different types of strawberry at The Pig, including the small but flavoursome white Alpine and wild varieties, which work well. You can adapt this to make one large cake if you prefer.

new forest strawberry cheesecake

Serves 8

For the base

(You'll need 8 stainless steel dessert rings measuring 7cm diameter x 4.5cm high)

- 200g McVitie's Hobnobs or digestives (best to use biscuits that aren't overly sweet)
- 50g unsalted butter
- 20g runny honey

For the cheesecake

- 350g Book & Bucket's Potter cheese (a soft cow's milk cheese), or any full-fat cream cheese
- 70g caster sugar
- 80g ripe strawberries, diced
- zest and juice of 1 lemon
- 150ml double cream

For the top

- 1-2 punnets ripe strawberries
- icing sugar
- zest and juice of 1 lemon

Break the biscuits into a food processor and blitz until fine. If you don't have one, place in a freezer bag and crush with the base of a pot or rolling pin.

Gently heat the butter and honey until just melted. Pour the hot liquid onto the crushed biscuits and, with a spoon, work in the butter mix until all the crumbs are coated. Divide the biscuit crumb between the dessert rings and press down with the base of a teaspoon. Chill in the fridge.

In a food mixer with the beater attachment (or large bowl and spatula), combine the cheese and 50g of the sugar – take care not to overwork it!

In a small pan, place the diced strawberries with the juice of the lemon and the remaining 20g sugar; gently heat until the strawberries break down to a pulp. Leave to cool completely.

In another large bowl, whip the cream with the lemon zest until it forms soft peaks – again, don't whip it too much or it'll split.

Using a spatula, gently fold the cream into the cheese in three or four stages. Mix in the chilled strawberry pulp (this adds a bit of colour and sharpness to the rich mix).

Remove the bases from the fridge. You can either spoon the cream cheese mix onto the base or you might find it easier to use a piping bag. Now, with a stepped palette knife (or the back of a spoon or spatula), level the mixture (if you run the spatula under hot water then dry it, it'll be easier to smooth).

Chill uncovered for at least 2 hours.

While it's chilling, hull and cut the small strawberries into halves and the larger ones into quarters, place in a bowl and sprinkle with a good amount of icing sugar and the zest and juice of the lemon. Cover and leave at room temperature.

When you're ready to serve, gently remove the cheesecakes from their moulds and decorate with the strawberries, then drizzle over the strawberry juices.

This is an indulgent treat for breakfast. You can chop and change the mix of fruit and nuts, depending on what you like and what's in your cupboard, but those lovely chewy caramelised clusters are what you want to end up with. The key thing to remember is to mix in any dried fruits at the end, because if you put them in the oven they'll get burnt and go crispy. This is delicious with natural yoghurt, milk or fresh fruit.

lex's luxury granola

Makes 25 portions

- 80g salted butter, melted
- 30g golden caster sugar
- 250g rolled oats
- 250g jumbo oats
- 45g desiccated coconut
- 70g mixed chopped nuts
- 70g whole blanched almonds
- 70g dried sour cherries
- 70g golden raisins
- 70g sultanas
- 100g soft light brown sugar
- 80g local honey
- 100ml maple syrup
- 80g salted butter
- zest and juice of 1 orange

Heat the oven to 180°C, 160°C fan (350°F), Gas Mark 4. In a large pan, melt the first lot of butter, add the sugar and stir till it dissolves. Add both lots of oats and mix into the warm buttery syrup. Spread onto a baking tray lined with parchment paper. Toast in the oven for 10-15 minutes till slightly brown and crisp. Weigh out the dried fruit separately from the nuts. In a pan, heat the soft brown sugar, honey, maple syrup, butter and orange zest and juice. Mix together everything (apart from the dried fruit) till combined. Grease and line two oven trays, spread the mix evenly and pat down slightly.

Bake for 8 minutes, remove from the oven and stir the oats to get an even colour. Turn down the oven to 170°C, 150°C fan (325°F), Gas Mark 3 and toast for another 10-15 minutes. Leave it to cool a little then check it's dry and crisp. Now break it up while still warm (otherwise it'll dry into a big clump!). You should have a few nice clusters, each around the size of a walnut. Now mix in the dried fruits. Allow to cool completely and store in an airtight container – although it probably won't stay there for long!

Most of us would recognise this as being similar to a crumble – a popular dish with the country folk of the 18th century as a way to use up overripe, damaged or a glut of fruit. Breadcrumbs feature in many dishes as a way of using stale bread so as not to waste anything. There are many versions, using any fruit available. Orange became a popular addition after it was introduced by the upper classes and so became fashionable.

rhubarb & rose betty

Serves 4

- 150g soft white breadcrumbs
- 90g unsalted butter
- 500g rhubarb
- 100g Demerara sugar
- zest and juice of 1 lemon
- ½ teaspoon rosewater
- fresh rose petals if available

Heat your oven to 240°C, 220°C fan (475°F), Gas Mark 9. For the breadcrumbs, remove the crusts, whizz in a processor and continue until you have 150g breadcrumbs.

Melt the butter in heavy pan, add the breadcrumbs and cook over a medium heat, stirring constantly to avoid burning, until light golden brown. Allow to cool in the pan and put to one side.

Top and tail the rhubarb, wash thoroughly and cut into even chunks 1cm thick. Spread on an ovenproof tray and liberally sprinkle with most of the Demerara sugar and the zest and juice of half the lemon (keep the remaining sugar, zest and juice for later).

Place on the middle shelf for 5 minutes, remove and allow to cool (you don't want it cooked through at this point). Reduce the oven temperature to 200°C, 180°C fan (400°F), Gas Mark 6.

Butter an ovenproof dish, check the rhubarb for sweetness and add more sugar, lemon juice or zest if you need it. Now add the rosewater (take care here – you don't want it tasting too much like Turkish delight).

Layer the breadcrumbs and fruit, starting with the fruit and finishing with a layer of breadcrumbs (if you have rose petals, thoroughly wash them in cold water, pat dry and place a layer on the fruit before the last layer of breadcrumbs). Sprinkle with the remaining Demerara sugar and bake for about 8-10 minutes until hot and the crumbs are golden.

Serve immediately with custard or cream – or both!

06

KING HENRY AND THE DELI BAR

HAMPSHIRE

IN THE WALL

THE PIG
in the Wall
ROOMS & BREAKFAST
WALK
THE
SOUTHAMPTON
WALLS

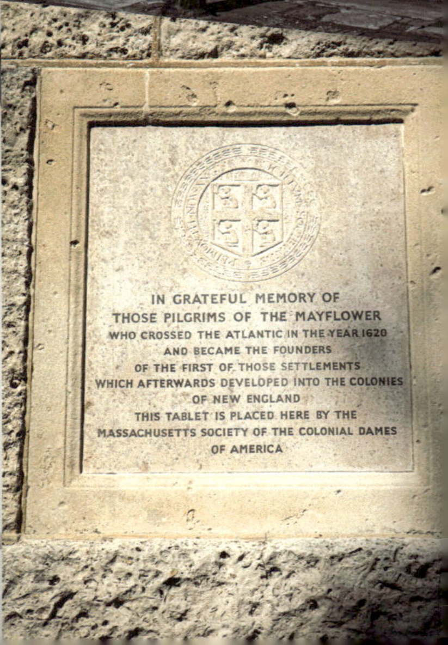
IN GRATEFUL MEMORY OF
THOSE PILGRIMS OF THE MAYFLOWER
WHO CROSSED THE ATLANTIC IN THE YEAR 1620
AND BECAME THE FOUNDERS
OF THE FIRST OF THOSE SETTLEMENTS
WHICH AFTERWARDS DEVELOPED INTO THE COLONIES
OF NEW ENGLAND
THIS TABLET IS PLACED HERE BY THE
MASSACHUSETTS SOCIETY OF THE COLONIAL DAMES
OF AMERICA

OPEN
BROCCOLI, BUTTERNUT SQUASH
POMEGRANATE
VEGAN SLAW

Robin: The Pig-in the Wall sits in the heart of the old city of Southampton, literally built into the city wall. Originally the site would have been on the quay itself, with ships anchored outside the door and a small boatyard in what is now our car park. This building started life as a residential house and would have felt very different then, with the hustle and bustle of the docks in front of it. Later it became a brewery and then a pub, before we rescued it. We also managed to purchase the adjacent house, which added a few more bedrooms, and we opened The Pig-in the Wall as a B&B with a deli bar in 2012. I love the heritage of the site, it's connected to so many hugely significant moments in British history.

ANSPACH PLACE
THE PIG
in the Wall
ROOMS & BREAKFAST
WALK
THE
SOUTHAMPTON
WALLS

HENRY V AND HIS TROOPS MARCHED THROUGH THE ARCHWAY NEXT TO US ON THEIR WAY TO AGINCOURT

We never really intended to have a city hotel, but when we came across this historic townhouse tucked into Southampton's ancient walls, we just fell for it. The Pig-in the Wall is a very different beast to our country hotels – no kitchen garden for a start, and not many pigs, chickens or sheep either, for that matter. But the same ethos applies: laid-back comfort in a handsome old house with a bit of a backstory and plenty of homegrown flavours to enjoy.

Unlike our other hotels, this one is B&B so, as well as breakfast, we just serve a range of salads and light dishes in the deli bar. Still, it means we make the most of the kitchen garden at the original Pig in Brockenhurst, which is only 20 minutes' drive away, not to mention some of the great local producers in Hampshire, Dorset and just over the Solent on the Isle of Wight.

What makes the place special is its extraordinary history – if you step outside, you can hardly move for heritage plaques! The archway next to us, the West Gate, originally led to the West Quay, which for centuries was the city's only commercial quay. It's through this archway that Henry V and his troops marched on their way to Agincourt in 1415. And a couple of centuries later, the Pilgrim Fathers set off on the Mayflower from a spot a short walk away. The Titanic also berthed here another few centuries on, but that is another story. Distinguished company, indeed.

The two most commonly used types of barley are pot and pearl. We use pearl in this recipe – because it's had the outer husk removed it cooks more quickly, but it's still chewy and deliciously nutty. Most people will be familiar with barley in a soup or stew, but it makes a great salad and can be served warm or cold.

pearl barley & aubergine

Serves 4 as a side

- 100g pearl barley
- 1 vegetable stock cube
- 1 aubergine
- 1-2 tablespoons rapeseed oil
- 2 sprigs rosemary
- 100g sundried tomatoes in oil
- 20g parsley, finely chopped
- 20g basil, finely chopped
- zest of 1 lemon
- salt and pepper

Place the barley in a pan, cover with boiling water, add a good pinch of salt and the stock cube. Simmer for 25-30 minutes until tender (you still want it to have a bit of bite).

Heat the oven to 220°C, 200°C fan (425°F), Gas Mark 7.

Dice the aubergine into roughly 3cm cubes, place in a mixing bowl, sprinkle in some salt, drizzle over the oil and mix well to ensure all the pieces are coated. Then place them on a baking tray lined with parchment paper and roast in the oven with the rosemary for about 15 minutes until the pieces take on a nice brown colour. Flip the cubes over and cook for a further 5-10 minutes.

Slice the sundried tomatoes (keep the oil from the tomatoes as we'll use this to dress the salad).

Once the barley and the aubergine are cooked, mix all the ingredients in a bowl and add 1 tablespoon of the oil from the tomatoes. Check the seasoning and add more salt and pepper if needed.

This is a lighter, fresher version of the traditional mayo-slathered salad, but once tried, lots of people tell us they prefer it. We add par-cel, which we grow at the hotel – it's a variety of celery bred just for the leaves and gives a distinctive flavour, but you can use flat leaf parsley if you prefer. You could add a bit of lemon zest for a citrus kick.

vegan potato salad

Serves 4 as a side

- 500g new potatoes
- ½ bunch par-cel (or flat leaf parsley)
- 3 spring onions
- 1 tablespoon wholegrain mustard
- 50ml rapeseed oil
- salt and pepper

Cut the larger potatoes in half and place in a saucepan of cold salted water. Bring the water to the boil then turn down to a simmer for around 20 minutes (until they slide off a knife easily when speared).

Drain the potatoes and place in ice-cold water briefly to stop them cooking further.

Finely chop the par-cel and the spring onions.

When the potatoes have cooled, mix everything together in a bowl.

This is a classic combo – the earthiness of the beetroot alongside the creamy mild goat's cheese. Rosary Goats Cheese began in Salisbury in 1988 and in 2014 took home the Supreme Champion Award at the British Cheese Awards. We grow a variety of beets, but if you aren't able to get golden beetroot, just stick with the traditional red varieties.

beetroot & goat's cheese

Serves 2 as a starter or 4 as a side

- 1kg mixed beetroot (golden and purple)
- 4 sprigs rosemary
- 1 whole garlic
- 200g creamy mild goat's cheese
- 100ml rapeseed oil
- salt and pepper

Place the beets in separate pans (to stop the colours bleeding) and cover with cold water. Put 1 sprig of rosemary and a quarter of the garlic in each pan. Bring to the boil then reduce the heat to a simmer.

Finely chop the rest of the rosemary and garlic.

Heat the oven to 200°C, 180°C fan (400°F), Gas Mark 6.

Once the beetroot is tender, drain, and when it's cool enough to handle, peel off the skin (you might want to wear gloves to stop your hands going pink!). Cut the beetroot into chunks and mix with the rosemary, garlic, oil, salt and pepper.

Spread on a baking tray and roast in the oven until the beetroot has nice crispy edges. Allow to cool slightly and arrange on a large plate. Crumble the goat's cheese over the top and serve.

Although this is a city hotel, we're lucky that we're so close here in Southampton to the New Forest and our kitchen garden there. This is one of our most popular deli salads, made with Brockenhurst's Tenderstem broccoli and squash. The pomegranate provides great colour and crunch.

roasted squash & broccoli salad

Serves 4

- 1 onion squash (or butternut)
- 1 tablespoon rapeseed oil
- salt and pepper
- 2 bunches Tenderstem broccoli
- 1 pomegranate

Heat the oven to 220°C, 200°C fan (425°F), Gas Mark 7.

Peel and dice the squash then mix it in a bowl with the oil and salt and pepper.

Spread it out on a baking tray and cook in the oven for around 20 minutes or until it takes on a good roasted colour.

Trim the base of the broccoli stems and place in a pan of boiling salted water. After 3 minutes drain and cool down by plunging into ice-cold water.

When both the squash and the broccoli have cooled, mix together in a bowl. If some stems are large, split them lengthways.

Cut the pomegranate in half and scoop out the seeds. Mix the seeds with the squash and broccoli, adding more seasoning if you need it.

With its sweet, nutty flavour and earthy aroma, Tunworth is probably the closest an English cheese gets to Camembert. Made by the Hampshire Cheese Company and named after the prettiest of hamlets, it's won countless awards. At The Pig-in the Wall we like to serve it baked whole with croutons, so get dunking!

baked tunworth

Serves 2

- 1 Tunworth cheese
- 1 sprig thyme
- 2 garlic cloves
- 2 teaspoons rapeseed oil
- a pinch of smoked salt

For the croutons

- 2 thin slices sourdough
- 25ml rapeseed oil
- salt and pepper

Heat the oven to 200°C, 180°C fan (400°F), Gas Mark 6.

With the point of a sharp knife, mark the top of the cheese with crosses – this will allow the oil, thyme and garlic to infuse the cheese while it's cooking.

Chop the thyme and crush the garlic in a pestle and mortar with the oil and seasoning.

Spread the garlicky mix over the cheese and bake for 10 minutes.

For the croutons, cut each slice of sourdough into 3, drizzle with oil, salt and pepper and cook at the same temperature for around the same time.

The Isle of Wight is a source of fantastic produce, and just a short hop away from us. IoW tomatoes are sweet and aromatic and the delicious Wild Island vinegar produced by Nuala Grandcourt gives just the right amount of bite in the dressing – if you haven't tried it, you really should! The halloumi we use is Smokey Burns Oak Smoked made by Book & Bucket in Dorset.

smoked halloumi & isle of wight tomatoes

Serves 4 as a side

- 1 smoked (or regular) halloumi
- 50ml rapeseed oil
- 400g mixed IoW tomatoes
- 200g rocket leaves
- 25ml IoW balsamic vinegar
- black pepper

Cut the halloumi into strips and halve them. Heat a little oil in a frying pan and fry the cheese for a couple of minutes on each side until it turns golden brown.

Cut the tomatoes in quarters or halves depending on size and shape and mix with the rocket in a bowl.

Once the halloumi has cooled a little, mix it with the tomatoes and rocket and place in a large serving bowl.

In a separate little bowl mix 25ml oil and the vinegar with a fork, then use this to dress the salad. The halloumi is fairly salty so taste the salad as a whole before seasoning and add pepper and salt only if it's needed.

07

HEARD IT ON THE GRAPEVINE

SUSSEX

IN THE SOUTH DOWNS
SOUTH-DOWNS WAY

MADEHURST

Robin: When I first set eyes on the extensive walled kitchen garden here, I knew this site would make the perfect Sussex Pig. The homely nature of the former dower house is, perhaps to many, the country house ideal. The main building is not that large, but the courtyard wing, converted stables and agricultural buildings give The Pig-in the South Downs its bedroom count. I've long been a fan of the developing English wine scene: indeed, our wine lists all feature some of the very best bottles made in England today, and we sell tens of thousands every year. So the idea of planting a vineyard wasn't such a huge leap once I'd discovered that the sheltered southwest-facing two-acre alpaca field in front of the hotel restaurant sat on the band of chalk subsoil that starts in Kent and ends in Champagne. Happy days!

THE CHALKY FOLDS OF THE SOUTH DOWNS HAVE FOUND ANOTHER VOCATION – AS ENGLAND'S NEW WINE HEARTLAND

There's a quintessential Englishness and gentle grandeur to the South Downs in this part of Sussex, with their sheep-dotted, chalky folds and hidden-away brick-and-flint villages. And they don't get much more hidden than Madehurst. You climb up the hill to the gates of Arundel Castle, with views across what feels like the whole of southern England, then take a sharp turn and suddenly you're in a secret valley of sun-dappled lanes, grazing horses, a cricket club, wheat fields and, finally, our newest Pig. We think – well we would, wouldn't we? – she's an elegant Georgian beauty of a house, up there on the hill, overlooking our first vineyard.

Sussex is wine country and we are thrilled to join the (slightly squiffy) party. There are some grand old piles around here – Petworth, Goodwood, Arundel – and although Madehurst was once part of a larger estate, the house feels homely, welcoming and gracious. The stables, chicken sheds and barns, and their little courtyards, make it feel like its own hamlet, with the big old cedar trees and a swing out front. This area has an impressive history of organic farming so we're enjoying making friends with our foodie neighbours. Nearby Goodwood was the first organically fed dairy farm in the country, and there are loads of smaller producers, cheesemakers, bakers and, of course, winemakers who Kamil, aka Professor Pickle, and his kitchen team are getting to know.

But our favourite thing late at night, after dinner, is to wander down to the vineyard and look up at the sky: this is one of only a handful of dark sky reserves in Britain and the stars are breathtaking. Then we have another glass and think about the grape harvests to come.

FIRST OF THE SUMMER WINE

Having the opportunity to plant my very own vineyard feels a little like being given my first train set. I suppose, over the years, in the back of my mind I had frequently thought about part-owning a vineyard or dabbling in winemaking. Not necessarily in the UK – although Rob at Castlewood does now make Devon Minnow Bacchus on behalf of Mark Hix and me – but perhaps I had imagined a few rows of Grenache nestling in the warm valleys of the southern Rhône or even joining forces with my mate Geoff Merrill in McLaren Vale in South Australia. But eventually, the opportunity presented itself quite by chance.

I have been an English fizz evangelist for many years – in fact, since 2014 we have been actively reducing sales of champagne by the glass at The Pigs, in favour of English sparkling wine. The quality has been so consistently good in recent years, I felt we should be supporting our native product. It was not until 2018, however, while opening The Pig-at Bridge Place in Kent, that I became really inspired by the leaps and bounds made with English still wines, in particular those of the super-talented makers from the vineyards of the Wine Garden of England. I was blown away by what was being achieved, not only with the arguably more predictable white wines made from Chardonnay grapes, but also the great rosé, amazing blanc de noirs (white wine from red grapes) and some luscious red wine from Pinot Noir. Fortunately, our forward-thinking sommelier teams at the Pigs didn't take any convincing to dedicate a sizeable chunk of their wine lists to these creations. They have searched the length and breadth of the UK to seek out the best offerings from Kent to Cornwall, Essex to Wales.

I am very proud of the passion these young wine professionals each have for their own wine lists. I can't think offhand of any other group of restaurants with such a commitment to English wine. I love hanging out, tasting and learning with our brilliant young wine team: it is a treat and a privilege and truly one of the best bits of my job. So, back to the vineyard story. Having bought the house, but delayed in the development of The Pig-in the South Downs due to various planning challenges, I was wandering around the grounds of the vacant house, thinking about how wonderful the view would be from the yet-to-be-built conservatory restaurant looking down the valley, across the hedgerows to those undulating Downs. My thoughts lingered on the perfectly formed two-acre field immediately in front of the building, and I began to think about those fantastic cellar-door restaurants overlooking their vineyards in the Napa Valley or Franschhoek in South Africa. Eureka! This chalky soil might just be perfect for a vineyard, I thought. A few calls to vineyard mates, a soil survey, the appointment of some great contractors and – hey presto – in May of 2020 our 4,000 baby vines were planted.

I want the entire team of sommeliers and gardeners to get involved in all aspects of our viticulture and viniculture, playing their part in the key decisions – as well as the all-important seasonal vineyard work. With some luck, by the end of 2022, we may get to taste our first still wines in barrel. I can't wait.

Cheers!
Robin

'SUGRUE SOUTH DOWNS IS MY EARLY MORNING AND WEEKEND JOB… I CALL IT A MARRIAGE MADE IN SUSSEX'

Dermot Sugrue, WINEMAKER

Dermot Sugrue is often described as Britain's best winemaker. It's a title he wears lightly, but one he's not prepared to concede too easily, either. By day, he is the head honcho at the Wiston Estate – the Sussex vineyard and winery owned by Harry and Pip Goring (photographed above with son and daughter-in-law, Richard and Kirsty, who now run the wine operation there) that makes, among other delicious libations, the award-winning Wiston and Goring wines. But it's perhaps his extracurricular work that has made him something of a cult winemaking hero. 'Sugrue South Downs is my early morning and weekend job,' says the Irishman of his eponymous wine company. 'I like to call it a marriage made in Sussex. Our wines combine grapes from the Storrington Priory vineyard in West Sussex and the Mount Harry vineyard in East Sussex – the two have a beautiful synergy.'

Dermot planted the vineyard at Storrington in 2006, the same year he left Nyetimber to join the Gorings in their winemaking adventure. He was asked to plant the vines by the monastic order of Catholic priests based in the town, and had no idea how successful the small plot could be. 'I knew the land had great potential to make a single vineyard wine,' says Dermot. 'It combined two great soil types – chalk and greensand – had excellent sun exposure and was well-protected from howling winds. The east-west orientation of the vines is different to almost all other English vineyards, a point of contrast I never really considered until the quality of the wines started to become evident.'

He named the vineyard and its signature cuvée, The Trouble With Dreams, after his favourite song by the American rock band Eels. Then in 2012, a disastrous year in which 'nobody in the UK picked anything', Dermot decided he needed a second source of grapes, so he took on Mount Harry vineyard, where 'the fruit delivers something more, a driving sense of purity that gives impeccable poise and definition to wines'. All Sugrue South Downs wines are Chardonnay dominant with some Pinot Noir added in for good measure. 'I'm always looking to express the individual fruit from that location,' he explains, 'and show a sense of place in the wines that I make.'

Here at The Pig we stock a number of the Wiston Estate wines and all four of the Sugrue South Downs cuvées: the aforementioned The Trouble With Dreams, a blanc de blancs called Cuvée Boz, the zero-dosage #Zodo and the absolute showstopper, Cuvée Dr Brendan O'Regan, a wine created to mark the centenary of Dermot's legendary great-uncle, a man who, among other notable achievements, invented duty-free and the Irish coffee. It's fair to say, we've got a lot to thank the pair of them for.

SUGRUE

This is very easy to make, and is just as good served in a large dish for a dinner party or for the family. At Madehurst we have seven mature fig trees: one Spanish Black, one Brown Turkey and five unknown varieties. One previous resident of the old Madehurst Lodge remembers her grandparents taking the figs to Covent Garden market to sell.

baked garden figs with honey & rosemary

Serves 2–3

- 6 figs
- 2–3 dessertspoons honey
- 100ml red wine or port
- 1 sprig rosemary (optional)

Heat the oven to 200°C, 180°C fan (400°F), Gas Mark 6.

Cut the figs in half lengthways and place in an ovenproof dish, seeds side up. Drizzle the honey over the figs then pour the wine over. Add the rosemary to the wine.

Cook uncovered in the centre of the oven for about 10 minutes and serve straight from the oven with ice cream.

An elaborate trifle with brandy, sherry, almonds and bay-flavoured custard, its name paying homage to the alcohol cleverly disguised inside the cake and custard. The traditional trifle made good use of stale cake soaked in alcohol, jam with no fresh fruit (this made it 'sloppy') and cream thickened with cornflour and almonds. Our recipe alters slightly from the original as we make the custard without cornflour and use well-drained preserved fruit from our grounds and fruit cages.

tipsy squire

Serves 4-6

- almond sponge (see recipe below)
- custard (see recipe below)
- 50ml brandy
- 200g fruit of your choice (we used cherries)
- 1 teaspoon caster sugar
- 50ml sherry
- 100ml double cream
- a little icing sugar (optional)
- 30g flaked almonds
- hundreds and thousands

For the almond sponge

- 75g room-temperature egg whites (roughly 3 egg whites)
- 100g caster sugar
- 50g egg yolk (roughly 3 egg yolks)
- 100g ground almonds
- 15g plain (or gluten-free) flour

For the custard

- 240ml double cream
- 1-2 small bay leaves (or, if you prefer, a vanilla pod, split)
- 80g egg yolk (roughly 4 egg yolks)
- 60g caster sugar

Heat oven to 200°C, 180°C fan (400°F), Gas Mark 6. Make your sponge. Whisk the egg whites and 50g sugar to make a stiff meringue; chill for later. Whisk the yolk with the remaining 50g of caster sugar until you have a pale, creamy texture. Sift the ground almonds and flour together, then fold in stages into the yolk mixture. Finally, fold in the meringue.

Grease a baking tray measuring 20 x 20cm, line with greaseproof paper and lightly grease this. Pour the mix onto the tray and gently spread evenly. Bake in the oven for 12-15 minutes, then allow to cool at room temperature before chilling in the fridge. When chilled, flip the tray upside down and release the sponge from the tray, then carefully peel the greaseproof away from the sponge, which should be moist and slightly sticky. Cut the sponge into 2cm squares; any leftovers can be frozen for future use.

For the custard, heat the cream and bay or vanilla. Thoroughly mix the yolk and sugar to a smooth paste. When the cream reaches boiling point, remove from heat and pour a little on to the egg mix, stirring constantly to form a smooth paste. Now add a little more to loosen it, then return to the pan of hot cream and vigorously whisk until blended. Return to a medium heat while stirring constantly until it reaches 82° C (or is thick enough to coat the back of a spoon). Remove the bay or vanilla, cover with greaseproof paper or clingfilm and allow to cool.

Put the brandy in a small pan with the fruit and the teaspoon of sugar. Warm through gently to soften, drain liquor into a bowl and add the sherry.

For the trifle, you can make it in individual dishes or a large bowl, but start with a layer of sponge, then a layer of fruit, then place another layer of sponge over that. Spoon over the boozy mix and liberally soak the sponge. Use the back of a spoon to push the sponge down so that it's even, and check that it's well soaked (if not, add more alcohol).

Next, coat the sponge with a good layer of custard, smoothing down with the back of a dessertspoon warmed in hot water.

Soft-whip the cream. If you want more sweetness, sift a little icing sugar into the cream. Either transfer to a piping bag and pipe onto the custard or, using a spoon, blob the cream straight onto the custard.

In a very hot oven, or under the grill, toast the flaked almonds until golden and allow to cool before standing them up in the cream. Finally, sprinkle the cream with the hundreds and thousands or coloured sugar strands.

THE FINAL COUNTDOWN

When we open a new hotel, there are years spent dreaming, planning then building. But it's in those last frenzied weeks that it all comes together. The place is teeming with people, all doing their jobs brilliantly: the decorators and carpenters adding the final touches; Judy – with the help of the ever-organised Amber – overseeing the arrival and installation of every piece of furniture, lamp or painting; gardeners finishing the planting... it's an exciting time.

Screen
PROPOSED ROOF PLAN
1:100
Hotel Development
architects
5298
1281

TEAM JUDY

Over the years, with each hotel we've opened, Judy's decorating style has evolved in keeping with the spirit of that house. It's fair to say that some of the quieter, muted shades are now mixed up with more dramatic moody colours, as well as some gorgeously patterned wallpapers and fabrics. One of Judy's favourites here in Madehurst is the lovely Arts-and-Crafts-inspired wallpaper in the hall from Chameleon Collection. 'I'd been waiting for just the right place to use it, and was so excited to find its perfect home,' she says.

Along the way, Judy has joined forces with some hugely talented collaborators, whose creations have become part of The Pig's design DNA. It's not just their work we love, but the whole ethos: homegrown, handmade and with a focus on vintage materials and sustainability. Sunbeam Jackie – otherwise known as artist couple Charlie and Katy Napier – design and make our vintage floral parasols in their 12th-century grain-store studio in Cornwall. A lovelier, sunnier couple you couldn't hope to meet. When they dropped Judy a note years back with pictures of early examples (they'd taken some prototypes to Glastonbury and people had gone wild for them), she immediately put in an order for The Pig-on the Beach. Working with Katy on colours and prints that match the mood of each hotel – in the case of Madehurst, inspired by vintage designs Katy found in the V&A – is one of the highlights of the design process and the day the parasols are delivered and installed is always exciting.

Similarly, working with Hilly Grumbar, of recycled-sari lampshade company Samarkand Design, is always a huge pleasure. Hilly is based near Tiverton in Devon, and after a career in overseas development, wanted to set up a company that combined her love of design and interiors with her commitment to a part of the world she knew and cared about – India. She buys vintage saris from all over the country (she is hugely knowledgeable about their design), then works with makers locally in southwest England to create the exquisitely handcrafted lampshades. 'I love going over to Hilly's studio,' says Judy. 'It's like an Aladdin's cave of all these gorgeous saris and fabrics; we have such fun.' Now Hilly's silk pleated lampshades are in all our hotels, and we couldn't imagine a Pig without them.

Hot

8PM:
10TH ANNIVERSARY STAFF PARTY

FIONA & TARA

LEX & BERTINA

ROBIN & JUDY

CHRIS

STEVE & WADE

LORA

JORGE

CHRIS

OLLIE & JO

MAIREAD

KAMIL

FRANCOIS

ANDY

JACQUI

MAIREAD & MARK

HAYLEY

GUY

OUR (NEXT) HEAD KITCHEN GARDENER

Dougie, whose middle name is Basil, was munching on raw veg almost before he could walk. His dad, Ollie, our group head kitchen gardener, lives and breathes his kitchen gardens, so as soon as Dougie and his big sister, Stephanie, could totter about, they were let loose in the family allotment to sample the produce. 'He just loves it,' says Ollie, 'especially raw beetroot and all the different kinds of tomatoes we grow.' Hardly surprising, given Ollie's feeling that we are simply looking after these gardens for the future: 'You should want to do justice to the gardeners who came before you and also leave them in a good state for the gardeners who'll come after,' he says. 'I strongly believe you're only a custodian of any garden for a while. You might be the head gardener, but you're not the head gardener for all time.'

Our approach to the kitchen gardens depends on what we inherit. Sometimes the garden is well established but neglected, in which case, we tend to stick with the original layout and planting scheme, and add some much-needed green-fingered TLC: improving the soil, getting rid of weeds and introducing some new varieties. Other times we have to start from scratch, creating a design, planting structure and overall scheme. But there are some basic ground rules: you need to work out which way is south, then ideally plant your rows to run from north to south to give them maximum exposure to the sun. Ollie likes to make his beds 50 inches wide for no other reason than it's the widest width for a gardener to comfortably straddle. Next, if you plan to have one, it's a good idea to think about where you're going to put your glasshouse. If there is already one there – like the 100-year-old glasshouse we inherited at The Pig-at Combe – plan the layout and especially the paths around it. If you're buying a new one, Ollie suggests an Alitex: 'They're pretty much the Rolls-Royce of glasshouses and make a lovely focal point.' But the most important thing is the soil, which is often light on organic content. Ollie mixes in a mushroom compost to create a fluffier soil and a healthier environment for invertebrates and root growth.

Other ground rules include placing your fruit cages in the sunniest part of the garden, putting your annuals – beetroot, beans, carrots – in raised beds, mainly for drainage. And beds for your perennial veg – rhubarb, sea kale, artichokes – can be sunk. Finally, be sure to stay on top of any weeds. 'There's an old adage: "One year's seeds makes seven years' weeds,"' says Ollie. 'Basically, if you let your weeds prosper they're going to be a real pain to get rid of. Of that you can be sure.'

This is head chef Kamil's famous salad, a summer dish that makes use of all our homegrown vegetables. The yoghurt dressing is light and fresh, and the basil and lovage add an aromatic bite.

tomato, spring onion & yoghurt salad

Serves 4 as a side

- 1kg mixed tomatoes
- salt and pepper
- 2 spring onions
- 80ml natural yoghurt
- zest and juice of 1 lemon
- 20g basil
- 20g lovage

Quarter or half the tomatoes depending on size and season with salt and pepper. Thinly slice the spring onions.

Place the yoghurt in a bowl and add the lemon zest.

Add in the tomatoes, spring onions, basil and lovage; check the seasoning. Add the lemon juice to your taste.

Another favourite salad and one that can be a side or the main event for a summer lunch. The freshness of the courgettes coupled with the earthiness of the cheese – from the Goodwood Estate – and the acidity of the lemon is a match made in heaven.

courgette ribbons, padron peppers & charlton cheese

Serves 4 as a side

- 1 medium green courgette
- 1 medium yellow courgette
- salt and pepper
- zest and juice of 1 lemon
- 8 padron peppers
- 1 tablespoon rapeseed oil
- 50g Charlton cheese (or another unpasteurised strongly flavoured hard British cheese), grated
- 1 red chilli, seeds removed and very finely sliced

Using a peeler, turn the courgettes into ribbons and discard the seeds. Season in a bowl with salt and pepper and the juice from a quarter lemon.

In a hot pan, fry the peppers in the oil for 3-5 minutes until slightly charred; season.

Mix both types of courgette with the peppers, the rest of the lemon juice, rapeseed oil, lemon zest and salt and pepper in a bowl and dress all the ingredients except the cheese. Serve on a plate, finely grate the cheese over the top, sprinkle on the chilli and serve.

We know that everyone loves their smashed avos with poached eggs for brunch, but with the controversy around the negative impact of avocado production, we felt it was damaging our sustainability ambitions and the time was right to find an alternative. Now we wouldn't go back! The smashed peas and soft egg yolk is a perfect combo – and if you like your morning eggs with a dash of spice, add a little chilli or Tabasco to taste.

smashed peas on sourdough with poached eggs

Serves 2 as a starter or for brunch

- 100g frozen peas, cooked in salted boiling water for 4 minutes then drained
- salt and pepper
- 50ml vegetable stock
- 20g butter, melted
- 1 large slice of sourdough
- 2 freshly poached eggs
- salt and pepper
- 1 fresh red chilli

Place the warm peas in a food processor and pulse until a rough purée is formed. Season and thin a little with some vegetable stock and butter.

Toast the sourdough and place on the plate. Gently heat the peas over a low heat. Poach your eggs and drain.

Spread the pea mixture on the warm toast and place the eggs on top. Season with salt and pepper and serve with a few fine slices of deseeded chilli.

SMOKERS' CORNER

Kamil, our head chef, is a smoking addict. Fish, meat, veg, fruit, salt, chillies, sugar – you name it, he'll smoke it. In fact, when he was supposed to be cooking dishes to be photographed for this book, we kept having to go and find him in the kitchen garden, tending to his smoker, which was rammed with goodies. It's easy enough to do this at home. People turn all kinds of things into smokers, from clay pots to oil drums. We even saw a red telephone box turned into a smoker in Somerset – but that's Somerset for you. Depending on what flavour you want, you can create your own mix of woodchips – Kamil tends to use a combination of apple, cedar, beech and oak.

This is a classic Pig dish and one we were keen to add our own twist to here in Madehurst. Charlie's Farm Shop is just down the hill in Bury, where Charlie Hughes's family have been dairy farming for three generations, and also producing rose veal. Veal has often been associated with unhappy farming methods, but it doesn't have to be this way. As Kamil likes to say: 'If you enjoy milk and cheese, you should also eat (well-reared) veal.' His point is that the unwanted bull calves of dairy cows can go on to live a productive life for up to another year, reared in large open barns. In this dish, the capers cut through the creamy flavour of the tender meat.

veal escalope with brown butter, capers & courgettes

Serves 2

For the veal

- 2 veal escalopes, each weighing 150–170g
- 50g plain flour
- 2 whole eggs, whisked
- 50g white breadcrumbs
- 1 tablespoon rapeseed oil
- 25g salted butter
- juice of 1 lemon

For the courgettes

- 2 medium courgettes
- 2 tablespoons rapeseed oil
- 50g butter, cut into cubes
- 2 teaspoons baby capers
- 20g chopped parsley
- salt and pepper
- a little grated Old Winchester cheese or Parmesan

If the escalopes are quite thick, you can place each between two layers of clingfilm and use a rolling pin to flatten them out.

Dip the veal in the flour, then egg, then breadcrumbs and place in the fridge.

Heat the oven to 200°C, 180°C fan (400°F), Gas Mark 6.

Finely dice the courgettes into small cubes around 0.5cm.

Put them on a baking tray with 2 tablespoons of oil and the cubed butter dotted over, and roast in the oven for about 8 minutes until golden brown. Add the capers and parsley and salt and pepper.

Heat 1 tablespoon of oil in a large heavy-bottomed frying pan and fry the veal for 3 minutes, add the remaining butter, then flip the veal and cook for another 3 minutes until golden on both sides. Squeeze over the lemon juice.

Put the veal on your plates, sprinkle with a little grated hard cheese (we use Old Winch or Parmesan), then add the vegetables and coat with the buttery sauce.

When Kamil arrived at The Pig-in the South Downs as head chef, he started to research lots of old Sussex recipes – and that's when he discovered that the county has just as strong a claim to the humble pasty as Cornwall. The Sussex version is made with lamb rather than beef, and served with a spicy, fruity brown sauce, Kamil's own homemade version of good old HP.

south downs lamb pasty

Makes 4

For the filling

- 1kg lamb shoulder
- 1 tablespoon Dijon mustard
- 4 banana shallots
- 4 garlic cloves
- 2 sprigs rosemary
- 500ml red wine
- 1 tablespoon rapeseed oil
- 250g celeriac, peeled and diced
- 250g swede, peeled and diced
- 2 large carrots, peeled and diced
- 2 medium onions, diced
- 3 garlic cloves
- 2 sprigs rosemary
- 4 sprigs thyme

For the pastry

- 510g plain flour
- 90g fine polenta
- 10g bicarbonate of soda
- 8g salt
- a pinch of onion powder
- 160g butter, melted
- 165ml warm water
- 2 egg yolks

For the fruity brown sauce

- 250g stoned Medjool dates
- 200g dried apricots
- ½ teaspoon each of ground allspice, ginger, nutmeg
- 300ml red wine vinegar
- 300ml white wine vinegar
- 4 apples, peeled, cored, grated
- 400g soft dark brown sugar

Season the lamb and cover with the mustard. Halve the shallots lengthways and place in the bottom of an ovenproof dish with the garlic and rosemary and put the lamb on top. Wrap everything well in foil.

We cook the meat at 88°C (190°F) overnight, otherwise you can start with the oven at 220°C, 200°C fan (425°F), Gas Mark 7 and cook for 45 minutes, then turn the oven down to 150°C, 130°C fan (270°F), Gas Mark ½, add the wine, cover with foil and return to the oven for 3 hours. Check the meat is tender and will shred easily. If not, return to the oven for 30-40 minutes. Remove the lamb from the oven tray and set aside. Skim excess fat from the juices and place the juices in a pan with the shallots and garlic; remove the herbs. Reduce by two-thirds. Using a hand blender, blitz the sauce.

Heat the oil in a large pan; add the veg and herbs. Sweat until they soften. Turn down the heat and cook without colouring for a further 5 minutes. Season to your liking. When the lamb has cooled a little, shred it into bite-sized chunks and mix with the veg and reduced cooking juices.

Make the pastry. Place the dry ingredients in a food mixer and, using the paddle, slowly add the butter and water. This should bind together quickly. It's best to roll out straight away, so make sure you have the filling ready.

Heat the oven to 200°C, 180°C fan (400°F), Gas Mark 6. Lightly flour your work surface and roll out the pastry to a thickness of 0.5cm. Using a plate as a template, cut 4 circles around 20cm in diameter.

Place the cooled filling on one half of a pastry disc, leaving 2cm free at the edge. Using the egg yolk and a pastry brush, egg-wash the edge and fold over to create a half-moon shape. Crimp together the pastry around the filling, ensuring it's well sealed. Egg-wash the outside and repeat with the rest of the pastry and filling. Bake in the oven for 15 minutes until golden.

For the sauce, chop the dates and apricots and place in a saucepan with the spices and vinegars; bring to a simmer. Add the apples and sugar and continue until the fruit is soft and the sugar has dissolved. Set to one side to cool a little. Place everything in a blender and blitz to a thick paste. This can be kept in the fridge in an airtight container for up to a month.

Serve hot with the fruity sauce and salad – it's also great cold the next day.

CAN HE DIG IT?

David Elton is the co-founder and a director of The Pig, and one of the many hats he wears is that of landscape-gardener-in-chief. The Pig-in the South Downs brought its own particular challenges. The first was a rather short, straight driveway and dense shrubbery, which David decided to reroute into an arc, cutting gaps into the shrubs 'to give a more interesting sense of arrival and open up a lovely view of the Downs'.

But the biggest task was transforming the courtyards and stable yards: 'The ground was solid hardstanding and there were hardly any areas where planting in the ground could happen. So we knew it had to be mostly container gardening, but on a scale that managed to create private gardens and terraces and a sense of privacy for the courtyard rooms.' The solution was to use huge galvanised planters, plus a range of old stone pots and agricultural-feed and water troughs. These established the separate areas and structure of the space, and were then filled with a mix of old olive trees and a wide variety of grasses, lavenders and thymes.

'The planting here is very relaxed,' says David, 'and we wanted to get that sense of flow from courtyard to courtyard. We grew most things from cuttings to keep our carbon footprint down, and dug up plants and replanted them in areas where it made more sense for them to be.' The walls of the house have been softened with virginia creeper, wisteria and jasmine mixed with recycled rambling roses and honeysuckle: a timeless English look. The team have also planted over a mile of new hedgerows.

It's amazing how quickly a garden can look as if it's been there forever with the right mix of planting and, crucially, some nice old containers. 'I was lucky to find 18 weathered staddle stones that all came from one farm. Similarly, the feeders are a bit battered, which breaks up any formality.' And the final touch? David's latest experiment is the stumpery, which is taking root in a dried-up drainage pond. Popular in Victorian times, stumperies are filled with tree stumps and logs, and provide a natural habitat for a wide variety of insects, frogs and toads. We're looking forward to seeing how it develops over the years.

GREENHOUSE GODDESS

Harpreet is our wonderful head therapist and works across all the hotels, helping with training and improving the quality of the treatments we offer. 'But I absolutely still do treatments myself,' she says, 'I wouldn't have it any other way. Massage is very much a part of Indian culture. I grew up in a household that believed in a natural and holistic way to heal the body, mind and spirit. I learnt so much of my massage technique from my family, in particular my father, by both giving and receiving massage daily. It's very much part of my DNA!' When we were about to open in the South Downs, Harpreet was there to oversee it all, and help set up our latest Potting Shed treatment rooms: 'At all the hotels, the treatment rooms are always set in gardens, very non-clinical and cosy, which is the Pig ethos.' But even by our standards, the rooms at Madehurst are quite unusual. You get to them through one of the greenhouses at the end of the kitchen garden, which houses a lovely gnarled vine.

'What I wanted to bring to The Pig and to all our team is the idea of learning to work from the heart rather than the mind and trusting your natural intuition. It brings authenticity to your work and, I think, makes you a better therapist.'

08

HOPS 'N' COCKLES 'N' ROCK 'N' ROLL

KENT

AT BRIDGE PLACE

SMOKED & UNCUT
2021 @ THE PIG-at Bridge
Director of THE PIG
Dressing

BRIDGE
BYRD BAKER
F.G.BYRD CONFECTIONER

Robin: This building has the most personal story of all for Judy and me. Just a small field of our livestock separates The Pig-at Bridge Place from the church where we got married, where our sons were christened and the graveyard where Judy's parents' headstone resides. Sadly, they both passed away before witnessing The Pig's arrival in their home village of Bridge, but they would have been very proud. In fact, we always say they can keep an eye on what we're up to from the graveyard! Judy spent her teenage years in the village, when Bridge Place Country Club (as it was then known) had a somewhat louche reputation. It was a thriving music venue, with the likes of Led Zeppelin and The Kinks playing early gigs there. Suffice to say, Judy's parents banned her from visiting this reputed den of iniquity – but girls will be girls and, as she says, she found far worse venues in nearby Canterbury. We've tried to keep the rock 'n' roll spirit alive at The Pig here, which has become the latest permanent venue for our Smoked & Uncut festivals.

Bridge Place Country Club
BRIDGE, NR. CANTERBURY
Phone : Bridge 208
★
Dance or drink, and if you wish, dine in this picturesque old manor. You may drink longer with our supper license. Ladies may come unescorted if they wish : Many do! There is an entrance charge of 5/- members, 7/6 guests, except where otherwise stated.
★
1968-1969
FORTHCOMING ATTRACTIONS
Fri. Dec. 13 YARDBIRDS (7/6 Members 10/- Guests)
Sat. Dec. 14 STATE ORGANIZATION
Sun. Dec. 15 CLOCKWORK SPONGE
Fri. Dec. 20 COURIERS
Sat. Dec. 21 SURPRISE NIGHT
Sun. Dec. 22 RENAISSANCE FAYRE
Tue. Dec. 24 Christmas The Carnival 8pm ________ ?
Two Groups, Fancy Hats, Masks etc. supplied.
Bar extension. (10/- Members 12/6 Guests)
Thu. Dec. 26 BOXING NIGHT BALL
Bar extension. (7/6 Members 10/- Guests)
Fri. Dec. 27 SPENCER DAVIS (10/- Members 12/6 Guests)
Sat. Dec. 28 URF
Sun. Dec. 29 STATE ORGANIZATION
Tue. Dec. 31 New Year's Eve Party 8pm ________ ?
Two Groups, Fancy Hats, Masks etc. supplied.
Bar extension. (10/- Members 12/6 Guests)
Fri. Jan. 3 P.P ARNOLD (7/6 Members 10/-Guests)
Sat. Jan. 4 TAKE FIVE
Sun. Jan. 5 CLOCKWORK SPONGE
Fri. Jan. 10 UNIT FOUR + TWO (7/6 Members 10/- Guests)
Sat. Jan. 11 ROAD RUNNERS
Sun. Jan. 12 HUNTSMAN
Fri. Jan. 17 SEARCHES (7/6 Members 10/- Guests)
Sat. Jan. 18 URF
Sun. Jan. 19 COURIERS
Fri. Jan. 24 LONG JOHN BALDRY (10/- Members 12/6 Guests)
Sat. Jan. 25 SURPRISE NIGHT
Sun. Jan. 26 CLOCKWORK SPONGE
Fri. Jan. 31 COURIERS
Sat. Feb. 1 RENAISSANCE FAYRE
Sun. Feb. 2 URF
Fri. Feb. 7 MOODY BLUES (10/- Members 12/6 Guests)
Sat. Feb. 8 BUTTONHOLE BAND
Sun. Feb 9 CLOCKWORK SPONGE
COMING SOON
Fri. Feb. 26 DAVE DEE, DOZY, BEAKY, MICK and TITCH
Fri. Mar. 9 BEN E. KING
Printed by the Elvy & Gibbs Partnership, 11 Best Lane, Canterbury
Bridge Place Country Club
BRIDGE, NR. CANTERBURY
Phone : Bridge 208
★
Dance or drink, and if you wish, dine in this picturesque old manor. You may drink longer with our supper license. Ladies may come unescorted if they wish : Many do ! There is an entrance charge of 5/- members, 7/6 guests, except where otherwise stated.
★
1969
FORTHCOMING ATTRACTIONS
Fri. Apr. 18 LONG JOHN BALDRY
Sat. Apr. 19 1981
Sun. Apr. 20 RESIDENT GROUP CANTERBURY TALES
Fri. Apr. 25 ★ BARRON KNIGHTS ★
Sat. Apr. 26 MIDNIGHT SUN
Sun. Apr. 27 RESIDENT GROUP
Fri. May. 2 ★ MOODY BLUES ★
Sat. May. 3 MARSHMALLOW TREE
Sun. May. 4 RESIDENT GROUP
Fri. May. 9 MIDNIGHT SUN
Sat. May. 10 1981
Sun. May. 11 RESIDENT GROUP
Fri. May. 16 FROM AMERICA DESMOND DEKKER and The ACES
Sat. May. 17 INNER CIRCLE
Sun. May. 18 RESIDENT GROUP
Fri. May. 23 THE FORTUNES
Sat. May. 24 MOOD REACTION
Sun. May. 25 RESIDENT GROUP
WHIT MONDAY, MAY 26th CLOCKWORK SPONGE
Fri. May. 30 P.P ARNOLD
Sat. May. 31 ROAD RUNNER
Sun. June. 1 RESIDENT GROUP
Fri. June. 6 STATE ORGANIZATION
Sat. June. 7 MIDNIGHT SUN
Sun. June. 8 CANTERBURY TALES
Fri. June. 13 SAM THE SHAM FROM U.S.A
THE WOOLY BULLY MAN HIMSELF
Sat. June. 14 1981
Sun. June. 15 RESIDENT GROUP
Fri. June. 20 COURIERS
Sat. June. 21 ★ COUNTRY COUSINS ★ (JOHNNY YOUNG FOUR)
Sun. June. 22 RESIDENT GROUP
Fri. June. 27 STATE ORGANISATION
Sat. June. 28 INNER CIRCLE
Sun. June. 29 RESIDENT GROUP
Fri. July. 4 CLIFF BENNET
Sat. July. 5 MOOD REACTION
Sun. July. 6 RESIDENT GROUP
Fri. July. [redacted] THE RONETTES
Sat. July. 12 CLOCKWORK SPONGE
Sun. July. 13 RESIDENT GROUP
Fri. July. 18 THE SEARCHERS
Sat. July. 19 JOHNNY YOUNG FOUR (COUNTRY COUSINS)
Printed by the Elvy & Gibbs Partnership, 11 Best Lane, Canterbury
Bridge Place Country Club
BRIDGE, NR. CANTERBURY
Phone : Bridge 208
★
Dance or drink, and if you wish, dine in this picturesque old manor. You may drink longer with our supper license. Ladies may come unescorted if they wish : Many do !
There is an entrance charge of 5/- members, 7/6 guests, except where otherwise stated.
★
1969
FORTHCOMING ATTRACTIONS
SUNDAY NIGHTS for a short while will have Resident or Surprise Groups performing.
Fri. Feb. 14 CLOCKWORK SPONGE + THE FUTT (7/6 Members 10/- Guests)
Sat. Feb. 15 RENAISSANCE FAYRE
Fri. Feb. 21 JULIAN KIRSH (6/- Members 8/- Guests)
Sat. Feb. 22 MARSHMELLOW TREE
Fri. Feb. 28 DAVE DEE, DOZY, BEAKY, MICK & TITCH (10/- Members 12/6 Guests)
Sat. Mar. 1 MOOD REACTION
Fri. Mar. 7 BEN E. KING (10/- Members 12/6 Guests)
Sat. Mar. 8 INNER CIRCLE
Fri. Mar. 14 JOHNNY YOUNG FOUR (COUNTRY COUSINS) (6/- Members 8/- Guests)
Sat. Mar. 15 GREEEN LIGHT
Fri. Mar. 21 FROM TRINIDAD 'DELROY WILLIAMS SHOW' (6/- Members 8/- Guests)
Sat. Mar. 22 THE STATE ORGANIZAION
Fri. Mar. 28 MOSAIC
Sat Mar. 29 THE ROAD RUNNERS
Fri. Apr. 4 (COUNTRY COUSINS) JOHNNY YOUNG FOUR
Sat. Apr. 4 CLOCKWORK SPONGE
Fri. Apr. 11 MOOD REACTION
Sat. Apr. 12 INNER CIRCLE
Fri. Apr. 16 RENAISSANCE FAYRE
Sat. Apr. 19 MARSHMELLOW TREE
Fri. Apr. 25 BARRON KNIGHTS (6/- Members 8/- Guests)
Printed by the Elvy & Gibbs Partnership, 11 Best Lane, Canterbury
Bridge Place Country Club
BRIDGE, NR. CANTERBURY
Phone : Bridge 208
★
Dance or drink, and if you wish, dine in this picturesque old manor. You may drink longer with our supper license. Ladies may come unescorted if they wish : Many do!
★
1968
FORTHCOMING ATTRACTIONS
Fri. Aug. 16 THE SEARCHERS (7/6 Members 10/- Guests)
Sat. Aug. 17 ★ HAWAIIAN ISLANDERS ★
Sun. Aug. 18 SHADES OF BLACK
Fri. Aug. 23 JOHNNY YOUNG FOUR
Sat. Aug. 24 WAYS AND MEANS
Sun. Aug. 25 PUFF WHEAT ORANGE
Fri. Aug. 30 P.P ARNOLD (7/6 Members 10/- Guests)
Sat. Aug. 31 RENAISSANCE FAYRE
Sun. Sept. 1 STATE ORGANIZATION
Fri. Sept. 6 ★ MIL. MOS MESSENGERS ★
Sat. Sept. 7 JULIAN KIRSH & HAWAIIAN ISLANDERS
Sun. Sept. 8 PIRATE BALL
Fri. Sept. 13 KEN COLYER
Sat. Sept. 14 VARIATIONS
Sun. Sept. 15 ★ DELROY WILLIAMS SHOW
AND BELLY DANCERS ★
Fri. Sept. 20 MOODY BLUES (7/6 Members 10/- Guests)
Fri. Oct. 4 IVAN CHIN'S WESR INDIAN STEEL BAND
Sun. Oct. 6 JOHNNY YOUNG FOUR
Fri. Oct. 11 COUNTRY COUSINS
Fri. Oct. 16 HUMPHREY LYTTLETON
Fri. Oct. 25 MOJOS
Sun. Oct. 27 ACKER BILK
Fri. Nov. 1 ALEX WALSH JAZZ BAND
Fri. Nov. 15 TERRY LIGHTFOOT
Sun. Dec. 8 KENNY BALL
PARTIES CATERED FOR
Printed by the Elvy & Gibbs Partnership, 11 Best Lane, Canterbury

ONE PART ROCK 'N' ROLL GLAMOUR TO ONE PART DARLING BUDS OF MAY, WITH JUST A DASH OF GOOD OLD ENGLISH NAUGHTINESS... BACK IN THE DAY, WHAT HAPPENED IN BRIDGE STAYED IN BRIDGE

Here, on the eastern edge of England, it certainly feels a long way from Harlyn Bay: getting on for 500 miles, if you travel as The Pig trots, taking a meandering route from hotel to hotel (more like 320 if you go direct). This is where the Kentish garden of England, all hops and berries and Darling Buds of May, rubs shoulders with the oysters, cockles and hipsters-on-sea of Margate and Whitstable, all just a stone's throw from Canterbury's ancient cobbled streets. It's a lively mix of cool-cat vibes, bucolic bliss and a revved-up food scene, with locals and out-of-town Londoners alike soaking it all up.

Which pretty much sums up Bridge Place. Looking like a stately doll's house amid the trees, this gorgeous brick manor has a rakish glamour all of its own. After centuries of life as the grandest of houses (it was built by the first manager of Dover Harbour, who was knighted in Canterbury by Charles II while the king was en route to London to claim the throne), Bridge Place began its unlikely reign as Kent's answer to Hotel California-meets-Studio 54 in the 1960s. Everyone from The Moody Blues to Desmond Dekker rocked out here, as the old flyers adorning the walls of the loos attest (history seems to have overlooked Clockwork Sponge, a big noise back in the day, apparently). By the 1970s, things had gone all glitter ball and flares, as locals flocked to show off their dodgy moves in the underground disco – the tales that emerged from Bridge were so racy they're still the talk of the village, 50 years on. In fact, we often have people coming for lunch, regaling us with stories of their misspent youth! We think that's all part of the appeal. Not exactly nights in white satin – we're more 100% Egyptian cotton people – but good times, for sure.

6.30PM: JOOLS & FRIENDS TAKE THE STAGE

Gibson

SMOKED & UNCUT
POPS UP
THE PIG - AT BRIDGE PLACE
Jools Holland

JELLIED
STEWED EE
James Golding
THE PIG

JUNKYARD PIZZA

All the Pigs serve their own versions of flatbread pizzas, but Bridge Place has a bit of a special set-up. Hidden behind a greenhouse in the kitchen garden is the wood oven, rigged up in its own little shack, built from all the reclaimed floorboards, doors and barn finds from the refurbishment of the main hotel and decorated with vintage London market fruit and veg signs. It's quite a suntrap down there, and on the right day, under the olive tree, you'd be forgiven for thinking you're somewhere more exotic than the good old garden of England.

DRINKS
CHAPEL DOWN SPARKLING BACCHUS (KENT, 29 MILES)
PIG LUI RED - WHITE - ROSE 125ml - £7.00 BOTTLE - £34.50
SIMPSONS RAILWAY HILL ROSE PINOT NOIR (KENT, 3 MILES) 125ml - £7.00 BOTTLE - £36.00
HUSH HEATH LIBERTY'S BACCHUS (KENT, 27 MILES)
BIDDENDEN GAMAY *SERVED CHILLED* (KENT, 27 MILES)
APEROL SPRITZ £10.00
GARDENERS 108 (NON ALCOHOLIC) £5.00
CHASE GB GIN + TONIC 40% £7.00
CHASE VODKA + MIXER £7.00 40%
KENTISH PIP SKYLARK CIDER
JAKE'S ROSE CIDER (TO SHARE) 8% £24.00
BIG DROP (LOW ALC) LAGER <0.5% £4.50
DRY DRAGON REAL KOMBUCHA 0%
EAGER ORANGE JUICE £3.00
BARDSLEY APPLE JUICE £3.50
COKE / DIET COKE £3.50
FEVER-TREE LEMONADE £3.00

We think celeriac is a bit of an unsung hero of the veg patch and we have lots in our kitchen garden at Bridge. Asterix is just one of the three or four varieties we grow. This dish makes a quick and easy starter, but it works equally well as a side with grilled or barbecued meat. Andy, head chef here, swears by the truffles found in Kingsdown by our local forager Nick, but good truffle oil works just as well. Be careful not to add too much though, as you don't want the truffle to overpower. Season well with plenty of black pepper.

truffled asterix celeriac

Serves 4–6

For the salsa

- 1 garlic clove
- 15g each of parsley, mint and basil
- 1 banana shallot
- 1 tablespoon capers
- 2 tablespoons extra virgin rapeseed oil
- zest and juice of 1 lemon
- salt and pepper

For the celeriac

- 1 celeriac, peeled and washed (you'll need 500g flesh)
- 2 tablespoons truffle oil
- 100g hazelnuts or cobnuts, toasted

For the salsa, finely chop the ingredients by hand.

Add to a mixing bowl and stir in the oil and lemon zest and juice. Season with a little salt and pepper.

Slice the celeriac as thinly as you can (use a mandolin if you have one). Lay out the slices flat on a plate, season with salt and truffle oil and leave to soften for about 20 minutes at room temperature.

Mix the celeriac with the salsa and spoon onto a plate.

For the nuts, heat a dry frying pan on a medium heat and add the nuts to colour slightly. Otherwise you can toast them under a medium grill for a couple of minutes, shaking the tray after 1 minute to colour them evenly.

Cool and crush the nuts by placing them in a thick plastic bag and bashing with a rolling pin. Sprinkle over the salad and serve. We finish ours with some slices of homemade pickled radish.

Kent is broccoli central – we grow loads in our own kitchen garden, but we also buy from Walmestone Growers. It was set up in the mid-1980s by John Aspinall because he wanted the very best for the animals at his zoos, Howletts and Port Lympne. We thought tigers preferred meat to broccoli, but maybe it's that good! This flan is perfect for a light lunch or picnic and is especially good served warm from the oven, with some pickled walnuts on the side for an extra kick.

walmestone growers broccoli & kentish blue cheese flan

Makes 6 individual flans

(You'll need dishes approx 10cm across and 2.5cm deep)

For the pastry

- 190g plain flour
- a good pinch of salt
- 90g unsalted butter or block margarine (plus a little extra for greasing), cut into small pieces
- 1-2 tablespoons ice-cold water

For the filling

- 180g broccoli, cut into small florets
- 1 banana shallot, finely diced
- 3 egg yolks (keep the whites for glazing)
- 3 large eggs, beaten
- 220ml double cream
- 150ml whole milk
- salt and pepper
- 180g Kentish Blue cheese (or other blue cheese), rind removed
- 1 tablespoon chopped chives

Heat the oven to 200°C, 180°C fan (400°F), Gas Mark 6 and grease your flan dish with butter or oil.

In a bowl, mix the flour and salt. Rub the butter into the flour until it resembles fine breadcrumbs. Add the ice-cold water until it comes together to form a dough (take care not to overmix). Finish by briefly kneading the dough until it's smooth and elastic. Wrap in clingfilm and place in the fridge. Leave to rest for at least 20 minutes.

Once chilled, remove from the fridge and roll out the dough onto a lightly floured surface until it's 5mm thick. Roll the pastry onto the rolling pin so you can lift it up, then lay over the greased flan dish. Ease it on gently, pushing it into the edges. Leave a small amount overhanging the edge of the dish. Using a fork, pierce the base several times to prevent air bubbles. Place a double layer of clingfilm or greaseproof paper larger than the flan case over the pastry. Fill with baking beans or rice. Blind-bake for 12 minutes until the pastry is set and not too brown at the edges. Remove the beans and using the egg whites, glaze the pastry to seal any holes and cook for a further 10 minutes. If any bubbles have formed, place the baking beans back on top to flatten it out.

Turn the oven down to 190°C, 170°C fan (375°F), Gas Mark 5.

Put the broccoli into a pan of boiling salted water for 2 minutes, then drain and plunge in ice-cold water to stop the cooking process.

Mix together the shallot, cream, milk and eggs in a bowl. Season with a little salt and freshly ground black pepper. Now you need to work quickly as you don't want the base to get soggy! Crumble the blue cheese onto the base, add a layer of florets, then sprinkle the chives on top.

Put the 6 dishes on a baking tray and place in the middle of the oven. Pull out the shelf and pour the liquid mix onto the base (it's much easier to handle this way). Bake for 20-25 minutes. If you give the tray a shake it should be just set, with a little wobble – but not runny. Garnish with a slice of pickled walnut and a selection of soft herbs.

This famous pudding from Kent has been eaten at cherry feasts and fairs since the 13th century. The idea is thought to have come to the UK with the Normans and is based on the French clafoutis. Kent's famous juicy black cherries – we get ours from Highland Court Farm – are perfect for this, but it can be made out of season with tinned cherries, thoroughly drained.

baked batter pudding with cherries & kentish farm yoghurt

Serves 4–6

(You'll need 6 x 12cm ovenproof dishes)

- 3 medium eggs
- 150g caster sugar
- 475ml whole milk natural yoghurt (we use the fantastic Otties Kent Farm Yoghurt) or crème fraîche
- 75g plain flour
- pinch of salt
- good squeeze of lemon juice
- 450g ripe cherries, washed
- 1 tablespoon cherry brandy (or normal brandy) – optional
- 1 tablespoon caster sugar
- a little butter for greasing
- icing sugar for dredging

Whisk the eggs and sugar for a few minutes.

Add the yoghurt or crème fraîche and combine slowly. Sieve the flour and fold in with the salt and lemon juice. Stone the cherries and place in a saucepan with the cherry brandy, if you're going for the boozy option, and sugar. Gently heat for 2-4 minutes to soften slightly.

Heat the oven to 200°C, 180°C fan (400°F), Gas Mark 6. Generously butter your ovenproof dish or flan tin. Spread the stoned cherries on the bottom and carefully pour over the batter. Bake for 15 minutes or until it's golden and set – it should have a little wobble.

Serve warm, generously dredged with icing sugar. This is lovely with cream or ice cream. (It can also be enjoyed cold, although it's a completely different pudding!)

AT THE HOP (PICKERS' HUTS)

One of the nicest things about Bridge Place is the way the Nailbourne, a tributary of the Stour, meanders through the grounds. It seemed like the perfect place to position the very Kentish version of our garden accommodation – the hop pickers' huts. Dotted along a hop-strewn boardwalk, with the river running alongside, they're the cosiest of dens, all with their own woodburners.

PIE
&
MASH

The sauce for this dish is a simple but delicious beef stew, known these days as a ragu – perfect for a weekend dinner when you have it simmering away all day, until the meat is fall-apart tender. We use Tom Sole's beef from Broxhall Farm – great quality and only three miles away. Deglaze the pan after searing the meat as the caramelised flavour and colour will blend into the sauce. This recipe can be adapted to use pork or lamb, with other aromatic herbs switched in, or even chillies. And if you really want to show off, make your own pasta – people are always ridiculously impressed!

pappardelle with braised short ribs

Serves 4

For the pasta

- 400g '00' flour
- 2 teaspoons salt
- 4 medium eggs
- 2 teaspoons olive oil

For the braised ribs

- 1kg short ribs
- 1 tablespoon rapeseed oil
- 2 medium onions, finely chopped
- 2 sticks celery, finely chopped
- 4 medium carrots, peeled and finely chopped
- 4 cloves garlic, sliced
- 5 medium fresh tomatoes, diced
- a sprig of rosemary
- a sprig of thyme
- 2 bay leaves
- 250ml good-quality red wine
- 500ml veal or beef stock
- 20g leaf parsley, roughly chopped
- 100g Old Winchester cheese

For the pasta, place the flour and salt on a board or kitchen surface and make a well in the middle. Gently whisk the eggs and olive oil with a fork.

Pour the egg mix into the well. Using your hand like a paddle, work the mixture for 5 minutes until all the flour and egg is incorporated and the dough is hard and springy. Clingfilm your dough and allow to rest in the fridge for 20 minutes before rolling.

Heat the oven to 170°C, 150°C fan (325°F), Gas Mark 3. Season the ribs well. Heat 1 tablespoon of oil in a heavy-bottomed casserole dish, sear the ribs then set to one side.

In the same pan, sweat the veg (apart from the tomatoes) on a medium heat, not allowing them to caramelise too quickly. Add more oil if you need it. Once the veg are lightly caramelised add the tomatoes, herbs and wine to deglaze the pan.

Return the beef to the pan, add the stock and cover with a lid. Put in the oven for 2½ hours. Check that the meat is soft and tender and falling off the bone (this can also be done in a slow cooker). Leave to rest in the cooking liquor for about 45 minutes then take it out and break it down.

Push the cooking liquor through a sieve and discard the veg, reduce the sauce until it coats the back of a spoon and add the beef back to the sauce.

If you have a pasta machine, use that as it's much easier! Roll out to a thickness of 2mm then cut into 2cm-thick ribbons.

Place the pasta in a large pan of salted boiling water and cook for 3-5 minutes till it begins to float but remains al dente. Drain and add the pasta to the beef sauce and, using tongs, combine everything together without breaking up the pasta. Serve with chopped parsley and grated Old Winch and, if you like, a few rings of pickled shallot.

angels on horseback

This classic oyster and bacon combo dates back to Victorian times. Happily for us at Bridge, we have Whitstable just down the road, world famous for its oysters – the natives have a much fuller, more intense flavour than imported varieties. Serve with devilled mayo or Tabasco for a spicy pre-dinner snack.

Serves 2 as a starter

- juice of 1 lemon
- 8 fresh oysters, removed from their shells
- 8 rashers smoked streaky bacon

For the devilled mayo

- 80g good-quality mayo
- ½ teaspoon paprika
- a pinch of cayenne pepper
- Tabasco – to your liking!
- 1 teaspoon lemon juice
- a good grind of black pepper

Heat the oven to 220°C, 200°C fan (425°F), Gas Mark 7. Sprinkle lemon juice over the oysters.

Lay the bacon rashers on a board and slide the back of a knife along each one to stretch it. Wrap a piece of bacon around each oyster. Place on a baking tray in the oven for 8-10 minutes.

For the devilled mayo, stir everything together. Serve your angels with this or just the Tabasco on its own.

---

cockle popcorn

This is one of our go-to nibbles, ready in 15 minutes. Cockles have a mild fish flavour so kids love them – they're like a posh fish nugget. Make sure the cockles are fresh and not the ones in a jar at the supermarket, otherwise this recipe won't work.

Serves 4 small portions

- 200g cockles, steamed and off the shell
- 100ml dry white wine
- 100ml water
- 1 bay leaf
- 100g plain flour
- 2 eggs, beaten
- 300g panko breadcrumbs (you can use fresh, but these are much nicer)
- zest and juice of 1 lemon
- 80g mayonnaise (homemade is best and not too difficult to make)
- 600ml vegetable or sunflower oil
- 1 lemon to serve, cut into wedges with seeds removed

Soak cockles in fresh water for 30 minutes to flush out any sand and silt. Discard any that are open or have chips out of the shell, then rinse again.

In a large pan, put the wine, water and bay leaf and bring to the boil. Add the cockles (chuck any open ones), cover with a lid and steam for 5 minutes. If any remain closed, cook for a further 2 minutes. If they're still shut, throw them away. Cool and remove the cockles from their shells.

Put the flour, eggs and breadcrumbs into three separate shallow bowls. Season the flour with salt and white pepper, add the cockles and coat well in flour. Using a fork, dip the cockles into the eggs a couple at a time, then into the breadcrumbs. Return the cockles to the egg and back to the breadcrumbs, to coat well. Mix the lemon zest and juice into the mayo.

Heat a heavy-bottomed pan with the oil to 170°C (375°F) or use a deep fat fryer if you have one. Cook a few at a time, as you will need to flip them over, so they're evenly cooked. Fry for 1-2 minutes until they're golden. Serve straight away with the lemony mayonnaise and a wedge of lemon.

If you think life's too short to make fishcakes, these beauties will change your mind. The garlicky, curried flavour is so different from anything you'd get in a supermarket – comfort food just doesn't get more comforting than this. We find that salmon, cod and smoked haddock make the perfect mix, but you can substitute other white fish for the cod. Serve with garlic mayonnaise and lemon and a crisp salad – then tuck in!

curried fishcakes

Makes 8

- 500g Maris Piper potatoes (peeled weight)
- 2 teaspoons rapeseed oil
- 1 medium white onion, finely chopped
- 3 garlic cloves, finely chopped
- 25g fresh ginger, peeled and finely chopped
- 1 red chilli, seeds removed and finely chopped
- 300g fish pie mix (salmon, cod and smoked haddock)
- handful of chopped coriander
- zest and juice of 1 lemon
- a good pinch of salt
- 150g plain flour
- 2 large eggs, beaten
- 200g fresh or dried fine breadcrumbs
- 600ml vegetable oil (for frying)

For the curried spice mix

- ½ teaspoon ground coriander
- ½ teaspoon ground cumin
- ½ teaspoon garam masala
- ½ teaspoon turmeric

Steam or boil the potatoes until soft, but not mushy.

Heat the oil in a heavy-bottomed pan and fry the onions. When they're soft, add the garlic and ginger and cook for a few more minutes.

Once the aroma of the garlic and ginger subsides, add the chilli and curried spice mix to the pan.

Cook on a low heat for 2 minutes then add the fish and cook for a further 5 minutes. Break it up a little but leave chunks. Now add the cooked potato.

Mix everything together and mash the potato roughly (the mix needs to be a bit lumpy). Season with the coriander, lemon zest and juice and salt.

Allow to cool, then shape into small cakes (around 100g each).

Put the flour, eggs and breadcrumbs into three separate shallow bowls. Coat each fishcake with flour, then dip in the egg, then the breadcrumbs. Set aside on a baking sheet.

Fry in a deep fat fryer at 170°C (375°F) for 6-7 minutes. For a healthier version, bake in the oven at 200°C, 180°C fan (400°F), Gas Mark 6 for around 20 minutes till nice and golden.

'KAMIL CALLED US SAYING HE WANTED SOME GEESE FOR CHRISTMAS... AND NOW HERE WE ARE'

Giles and Kate Campbell, LONGLAND FARM

Giles and Kate Campbell first appeared on our radar a couple of years ago when we spotted them leading a flock of 70 energetic geese through the nearby village of Bishopsbourne. They were moving their young goslings to a larger field for the summer, and half of the village was in attendance, cheering them on. This was bucolic Blighty at its best – the local vicar even blessed the birds as they waddled past the church.

Kamil (then head chef at Bridge, but now at The Pig-in the South Downs) was among the onlookers, and if anyone can spot a healthy, happy goose, it's him. 'A few months later, Kamil called us, saying he was looking for some geese for the Christmas period,' remembers Giles. 'Well, they certainly shot off the menu. So he ordered some of our ducks, and now here we are – The Pig is one of our best customers.'

At Longland Farm, on the outskirts of Elham, the Campbells have their own hatchery and slaughterhouse, so their poultry has the most stress-free life possible. They rear their birds slowly in large grassland fields, allowing them to mature and develop a better bone structure and a richer flavour. Their ducks are grown up to 16 weeks, whereas supermarket ducks are grown to only seven weeks and six days.

'If you want to produce a decent duck you ought to game-hang it,' explains Giles. 'This means dry-plucking by hand, one bird at a time, before waxing it and letting it set. You then strip off the wax to remove any fluff and hang it in the chiller for up to a week.' Not only does this intensify the flavour, it allows you to age the bird further, creating meat with a colour more akin to beef, that is juicy

Longland Farm is one of only a handful of farms in the country where the ducks, geese and chickens are outside all year round, so we're really lucky to have it on our doorstep. The work that's put into rearing the birds gives them an amazing flavour. The use of a spice rub and the sweet roasted plums help to cut through the rich fattiness of the meat.

spiced longland farm duck breast

Serves 2

- 1 tablespoon cumin seeds
- 1 tablespoon coriander seeds
- 1 tablespoon fennel seeds
- 2 star anise
- 200g Hoaden Court plums (or foraged ripe plums)
- 100ml good-quality red wine
- 200ml veal stock (or other rich meat stock)
- 2 duck breasts, trimmed and scored
- salt and pepper

Toast the spices in a dry frying pan then blend the mix to a fine powder in a spice grinder. If you don't have one, you can do it the old-fashioned way with a pestle and mortar. Set the spices aside.

For the sauce, halve the plums and remove the stones. In a hot pan, colour the plums and once they're caramelised on both sides, add the red wine. Let the alcohol cook out and then add the stock. Reduce the sauce till it can coat the back of a spoon.

Season the duck with salt, pepper and a generous amount of the spice mix.

Starting with a cold, non-stick pan, add the duck to the pan, skin-side down, and render the fat slowly on a medium heat (this will take about 5 minutes). Once the fat's rendered down and the skin is crispy, flip the breasts and sear the meat side (another 4-5 minutes for medium rare). Take off the heat and leave to rest in the pan.

Slice the breasts and add any juices from the meat to the plum sauce. Serve with the plum sauce and side dishes of your choice.

THE VELVET UNDERGROUND

When Judy planned the interiors for Bridge Place, she channelled her inner rock chick, with lots of deep velvet sofas, beaded and tasselled lampshades and lush moody colours. It's a house full of naughty nooks, wood-panelled bedrooms and snugs for late-night canoodling. The wooden arched door in the sitting room was the entrance to the old 1960s nightclub.

R:ZINC
IN:A:
TR:CIN
RR:CARB
B:OPT
ALOM:SAC
POT:CI
P:TART
AVAND
Q:CINNA

Index

Cookery notes

The Pig's style of cooking is relaxed and in most of our recipes if we suggest a slosh or a handful, the exact amount won't be too critical. When the amounts are more critical, we give exact measurements.

Eggs: medium-sized, unless otherwise stated, free range/organic
Meat: use the best you can afford; free-range, organic and local if possible. If you can, use a butcher rather than a supermarket
Fish: we buy local fish; you should make sure it is sustainably sourced

Lemons: use unwaxed lemons for zesting
Wine: good enough to drink is good enough to cook with
Cheese: we serve local cheeses, most of which can be bought online. Otherwise, use the alternatives given
Garlic: peeled and crushed, unless otherwise specified

Herbs: we grow our own; any fresh herbs will do
Fruit vinegar: we use local fruit vinegars, which you can buy online. Otherwise, cider vinegar is the closest alternative
Salt: we use sea salt flakes, such as Cornish Sea Salt
Pepper: freshly ground black pepper

The Pig cast and crew

Darcy A'Barrow, Waiter. Natalie Abbott, Budding Entrepreneur. Paris Abley, Waiter. Ella Adams, Therapist. Fraser Aitken, Commis Chef. Zeynep Akbulut, Room Attendant. Natalie Albery, Reservations Supervisor. Daniel Alecu, Kitchen Porter. Joshua Allen, Sous Chef. Ben Alton, Kitchen Gardener. David Ambrus, Kitchen Porter. Victoria Amos, Waiter. Lukas Andr, Deputy General Manager. Paige Apetino, Receptionist. Henry Applegate, Apprentice. Heidi Arnall, Head Therapist. Adele Atkinson, Therapist. Terry Attwood, Demi Chef de Partie. Charlotte Attwood, Therapist. Jake Avery, Apprentice. Nigel Bacon, Junior Sous Chef. Paula Bacon-Wilkes, Room Attendant. Freya Baddeley, Waiter. Jeremy Baker, Commis Chef. Maria Baker, Therapist. Victoria Bancroft, Reception Manager. Jamie Banner, Deputy General Manager. Natasha Banner, Smoked & Uncut Assistant. Toni Barker, Demi Chef de Partie. Rosie Barker, Duty Manager. Christine Barnden, Room Attendant. Niall Barnett, Budding Entrepreneur. Archie Barron, Kitchen Porter. Isobel Bartlam, Waiter. Alexa Bartlett-Woodnutt, Pig Book Recipe Queen. Vivienne Barton, Head Housekeeper. Adrian Barton, Kitchen Porter. Tim Batchelor, Smoked & Uncut Co-ordinator and Bar Wizard. Mark Baxter, Groundsman. Max Bayles, Waiter. Trudie Bean, Room Attendant. Oskar Beim, Junior Sous Chef. Andrew Bell, Chef de Partie. Melissa Bellm, Receptionist. Remi Bennett, Assistant Bar Manager. Chanay Bennett, Room Attendant. Edward Benson, Waiter. Stephanie Beresforde, Restaurant Manager. Simon Berry, Chef de Partie. Maria Bertiz, Therapist. Samantha Beukes, Accounts Assistant. Sarah Bilson, Room Attendant. Rebecca Bird, Bartender. Kyle Bishop, Apprentice. Suzi Black, Administrator. Charlotte Blackmore, Apprentice. Peter Blake-Burke, Night Porter. Ross Blandford, F&B Night Porter. Chloe Blanks, Waiter. Radoslaw Blaszka, Regional Maintenance Manager. Nathan Blatchford, Chef de Rang. Garry Block, Night Manager. Leon Bloy-Neve, Linen Porter. Simone Blunden, Therapist. Tadeusz Bomersbach, Housekeeper. Kristian Bonev, Chef de Partie. Charlotte Bonham, Senior Chef de Partie. Laura Bonney, Room Attendant. Sarah Borman, Administrator. William Bottomley, Kitchen Porter. Francois Bourde, Hotel Manager. Yangchen Bowe, Room Attendant. Mary-Anna Bowen, Reception Manager. Danny Bowles, Senior Chef de Partie. Tean Bradford, Bar Manager. Jay Brady, Chef de Partie. Heather Brennan, Demi Chef de Partie. Adam Bristow, Head Chef. Victoria Bristow, Training Administrator and Content Developer. Charlotte Brockbank, Room Attendant. Elle Brooke, Receptionist. Sarah Brosnan, Gardener/Animals. Ayshea Brown, Reservationist. Stuart Browne, Night General Assistant. Lotti Bruce, Head of Marketing. Daniel Buck, Bartender. Krista Buckley, Kitchen Gardener. Finn Budd, Kitchen Porter. James Bugler, Linen Porter. Simin Bui, Kitchen Porter. Luke Bull, Assistant Head Housekeeper. Anne Bunting, Reservationist. Charles Burroughs, Grounds Assistant. Katherine Burton, Payroll Administrator. Archie Bush, Waiter. Leanne Bush, Therapist. Barry Butler, Driver. Anita Butler, Gardener. Jose Cacin, Chef de Partie. Eleanor Canning, Restaurant Supervisor. Loren Capel, Reservationist. Emile Caplin, Bar Supervisor. Izabella Carmen, Waiter. Nelson Carnell-Mckean, Apprentice. Shane Carr, Kitchen Porter. Bobby Carroll, Assistant Bar Manager. Ben Carter, Assistant Management Accountant. Harry Cartwright, Sous Chef. Imogen Chamberlain, Waiter. Reginald Chambers, Kitchen Porter. Grace Chapman, Chef de Rang. Wioletta Chara, Floor Supervisor. Christopher Charles, General Manager. Emma-Jay Chellingworth, Housekeeping Supervisor. Francisco Chilet-Olmos, Senior Head Kitchen Gardener. Alina Chis, Bartender. Chantal Chorley, Room Attendant. Bethany Chown, Budding Entrepreneur. Neil Churcher, Night Porter. Amanda Churcher, F&B Night Porter. Paulina Cimoch, Housekeeper. Georgia Clark, Demi Chef de Partie. Megan Clarke, Payroll Administrator. William Clarke, Trainee Sommelier. Julie Clayton, Room Attendant. Karen Clayton, Therapist. Edward Clear, Chef de Partie. Antonia Clemens, Senior Therapist. Thomas Clements, Waiter. Hannah Clough, Waiter. Brittany Coleman-Smith, Waiter. Peter Collings, Demi Chef de Partie. Joseph Collins, Nursery Supervisor. Hannah Collins, Receptionist. Toby Colmer, Bartender. Michael Conniff, Kitchen Porter. Jonathan Constance, Kitchen Assistant. Emma Conway, Room Attendant. Jennifer Coombes, Senior Therapist. Kelly Cooper, House Manager. Bradley Corbin, Waiter. Cameron Corrick, Commis Chef. Maria Costa, Room Attendant. Isabel Costa Imale, Room Attendant. Morgan Coster, Waiter. Abbie Cottrell, Therapist. Richard Couch, Night Duty Manager. Maisie Court, Room Attendant. Laura Cousens, Room Attendant. Alex Coutts, Head Kitchen Gardener. Aitor Covian, Senior Chef de Partie. Hannah Cowan, Waiter. Jessica Cowing, Breakfast Chef. Eliza Cox, Trainee Sommelier. Natalie Cox, Room Attendant. Tara Crabb, Hotel Director. Sarah Crane, Chef de Partie. Joanne Cranwell, General Assistant. Jenny Cregg, Purchase Ledger Manager. Cristian Croker, Waiter. Isobel Croly, Bar Supervisor. Frederick Crouch, Chef de Rang. Lorand Csontos, Night General Assistant. Michael Cullen, Kitchen Porter. Timothy Cullinane, Senior Sous Chef. Camilla Cummins, Waiter. Stuart Cunningham, Deputy General Manager. Poppy Curley-Smith, Bartender. Maria Eugenia Curto, Commis Sommelier. James Cusselle, Head Sommelier. Megan Daniel, Housekeeper. Amy Daponte, Waiter. Holly Daponte, Waiter. Lewis Dark, Waiter. Sarah Davies, Payroll Supervisor. James Davies, Grounds Assistant. Ella Davies, Waiter. Amy Davies, Chef de Rang. Gregory Davies, Kitchen Porter. Alice Davies, Bartender. Luis Davila, Lobster Shed Manager. Nichola Davis, Apprentice. Adam Davis, Bartender. Rosemary Dawkins, Chef de Partie. Joseph Deakin, Sommelier. Ben Deam, Chef de Rang. Ella Debenham, Room Attendant. Peter Deeks, Chef de Partie. Melanie Den-McKay, Therapist. John Derbyshire, Night Porter. Eryk Deryniowski, Kitchen Porter. Emma Desborough, Group Financial Controller. Joe Devine, Gardener. Evie Dewhurst, Chef de Rang. Zack Dickson, Waiter. James Dixon, Assistant Restaurant Manager. Madison Dodd, Chef de Partie. Szymon Doliwa, Commis Chef. Vlada Dolotova, Night Manager. Ruby Donadel, Room Attendant. Lawrence Dougall, Commis Chef. Flynn Dougall, Kitchen Porter. Charlotte Douglas, Waiter. Raymond Dowdney, Assistant Maintenance Manager. Richard Dowdney, Budding Entrepreneur. Daisy Downs, Chef de Rang. Molly Dowson McGill, Waiter. Lara Drew, Room Attendant. Katie Drinkwater, Budding Entrepreneur. Christopher Drodge, Hotel Director. Toby Dronfield, Linen Porter. Alexandra D'Souza, Bartender. Grace Duckerin, Waiter. Johanna Dulieu, Bar Manager. Jessica Dunham, Waiter. Nadia Dunn, Waiter. James Dutton, Gardener. Shannon Dyke, Bartender. Gillian Eaton, Receptionist. Joshua Edmond, Junior Sous Chef. Aaron Edwardes, Chef de Partie. Ellie Edwards, Assistant Reception Manager. Oliver Edwards, Gardener. Duncan Edwards, Night Duty Manager. Sarah Edwards, Host. Alexzandria Edwards, Receptionist. Poppy Edwards Smith, Waiter. Ella Eitel, Waiter. Stephen Elgie, General Assistant. Lola Elliot, Waiter. Abby Elliott, Chef de Rang. Patrick Ellis-Forrester, Chef de Partie. David Elton, Green-fingered Co-founder and Marketing Guru. Benjamin Emerson, Senior Chef de Partie. Catherine Endean, Head Therapist. Scarlett English, Head Groundsperson. Imogen English, Room Attendant. Christine English, Room Attendant. Jack Evans, Trainee Sommelier. Tabitha Evans, Waiter. Freya Fairbanks, Chef de Partie. Benjamin Falinski, Waiter. Bianka Farkas, Waiter. Matthew Farmer, Bartender. Oliver Farrant, Gardener. Andrew Feasby, Head Chef. Correy Feeney, Junior Sous Chef. Haley-Jane Ferguson, Bartender. Matilda Ferguson, Waiter. Renato Silvio Ferreira Mendes, Junior Sous Chef. Charlotte Fleet, Receptionist. Andrew Fleming, Kitchen Porter. Nathaniel Florence-Wratten, Apprentice. Agnieszka Florkiewicz, Room Attendant. Jose Bautista Forner Arin, Maintenance Manager. Victoria Forster, Therapist. Harriet Forsyth, Accounts Assistant. Lily Foster, Waiter. Joanna Foulkes, Administrator. Evie Fowler, Folly Supervisor. Sophie Fowler, Bartender. Laurie Fox, Waiter. Vivian Francis, Kitchen Porter. Rodney Franco, Bartender. Giuliana Franzese-Henry, Housekeeper. Serena Frazer, Assistant Restaurant Manager. Guy Freedman, Hotel Director. Ben Fuller, Commis Chef. Ian Fumagall, Maintenance Assistant. Jessica Fuoco, Bartender. Laura-Jane Fuoco, Waiter. Isobelle Gamble, Waiter. Sophia Gamble, Waiter. Paul Gamble, Breakfast Chef. Alexia Garcia Ferrer, Reception Manager. Emma Gascoine, Reservationist. Kerry Gavriilidi, Room Attendant. Daniel Gavriilidis, Head Chef. Michal Gawronski, Night Supervisor. Sarah Elgie, Business Development. Jidy George, Demi Chef de Partie. Jorge Gertrudes, Regional Operations Director. Liliana Gertrudes, Waiter. Harpreet Ghatora, Wellness Guru. Ioana Gheorghe, Room Attendant. Matthew Gibb, Room Attendant. Jasmine Gibbs, Therapist. Slawomir Gil, Maintenance Engineer. Magdalena Gil, Assistant Head Housekeeper. Laura Giles, Assistant Head Sommelier. Chloe Gill, Receptionist. Matthew Gill, Waiter. Laetitia Gill , Assistant Deli Manager. Sue Gillatt, Head Housekeeper. Jenna Glazier, Room Attendant. Mairead Gleeson, Hotel Director. Bethany Goddard, Commis Chef. Jonathan Golder, Assistant Restaurant Manager. James Golding, Chef Director. Larabella Gonzalez-Sol, Waiter. Megan Goodwin, Room Attendant. James Gosley, Breakfast Chef. Jonathan Gotthardt, Senior Duty Manager. Ellie Govier, Waiter. Samuel Govinden, Apprentice. Daniel Granger, Waiter. Christopher Grattan, Maintenance Apprentice. George Gray, Kitchen Porter. Etta Greenhalgh, Waiter. Abigail Greenslade, Head Therapist. Chloe Greet, Room Attendant. William Griffith, Waiter. John Griffiths, Night General Assistant. Colin Grimley, Kitchen Porter. Kerrie Grundy, Bar Manager. Louise Guille, Senior Chef de Partie. Cara Gumbrell, Receptionist. Benjamin Guy, Pastry Chef de Partie. Edward Gwernan-Jones, Chef de Partie. Sophia Gyger, Restaurant Manager. Nicola Hadaway, Senior Room Attendant. Jamie Hadwick,

Demi Chef de Partie. Tina Hafey, Room Attendant. Euan Haines, Senior Chef de Partie. Georgina Haines, Receptionist. Joanne Hallett, Room Attendant. Rupert Halls, Kitchen Porter. Jodie Hambling, Head Waiter. Stephen Hammond, F&B Night Porter. Matthew Hancock, Chef de Partie. Ella Hands, Apprentice. Luke Harbor, Head Sommelier. William Hardwick, Waiter. Joseph Hardwick-Adams, Kitchen Porter. Steve Harley, Senior Chef de Partie. Gemma Harriott, Waiter. Peter Harris, Head Kitchen Gardener. Darryl Harris, F&B Operations Manager. Sarah Harris, Therapist. Madeleine Harris, Waiter. Jack Harrison, Waiter. Jordon Harrison, Kitchen Porter. Jamie Harrison, Waiter. James Hart, Kitchen Porter. Shannon Harvey, Group People, Learning & Development Manager. Ruby Harvey, Waiter. Lottie Harvey, Apprentice. Isabel Hauxwell, Waiter. Jacob Hawkins, Apprentice. Chloe Hayhurst, Kitchen Gardener. Anna Hayward, Head of Sales. Mark Healey, Linen Porter. William Heathcote, Bartender. Jacek Helbik, Head Housekeeper. Chelsea Hendrick, Commis Sommelier. Thomas Henrich, Kitchen Porter. Emilia Hermelin, Receptionist. Violet Herrington, Waiter. Angel Hervas, Kitchen Assistant. Garth Hewitt, House Manager. Charlotte Hicks, Apprentice. Hannah Hide, Waiter. Annabel Hill, F&B Supervisor. Rex Hill, Kitchen Porter. Georgina Hilliard, Reception Supervisor. Nelly Hillier, Waiter. Bill Hillier, Waiter. Katie Hillier, Bartender. Emily Hillier, Receptionist. David Hoare, Junior Sous Chef. Alice Hockley, Waiter. Amanda Hodson, Therapist. Jules Holden, Waiter. Malo Holden, Waiter. Clarisse Holden, Waiter. Sarah Holden, Hotel Director. Chloe Holliday, Budding Entrepreneur. Donna Holliday, Room Attendant. Tom Holloway, Senior Sous Chef. Millie Holman, Waiter. Marie-Theres Holtmann, Senior Assistant Restaurant Manager. Martin Hooper, Head Kitchen Porter. Rebecca Hooton, Administrator. Liam Hopes, Kitchen Gardener. Alice Hopgood-Tavener, Assistant Restaurant Manager. Nadia Hopkins, Reservationist. Hayley Hopkins, Chef de Rang. Emily Horman, Head Therapist. Rodger Horne, Breakfast Chef. Nathan Hoskins, Kitchen Gardener. Dean Howell, Night Porter. Natasha Hughes, Senior Chef de Partie. Sebastian Hughes, Bartender. Gemma Hughes, Assistant Head Housekeeper. Abigail Hughes, Kitchen Assistant. Samuel Humphreys, Kitchen Gardener. Jack Humphries, Senior Pastry Chef de Partie. Isabelle Hunt, Bartender. Karen Hunt, Therapist. Jessica Hunter, Waiter. Rebecca Huntley, Kitchen Gardener. Poppy Hurst, Waiter. Ollie Hutson, Group Head Kitchen Gardener. Judy Hutson, Interior Designer. Robin Hutson, General Dogsbody. Stefka Ilieva, Assistant Head Housekeeper. Harriet Inglis, Grounds Assistant. Hannah Isherwood, Assistant Lobster Shed Manager. Agata Jach, Room Attendant. Oliver Jackson, Senior Chef de Partie. Kay Jakeman, Assistant Head Housekeeper. Antony Jakeman, Maintenance Assistant. Tristan Jarvis, Waiter. Anastazja Jasiorska, Housekeeper. Edyta Jaworska, Kitchen Gardener. Ellen Jeffrey, Budding Entrepreneur. Franziska Jenetzky, Receptionist. Vikki Jerram, Finance Director. James Jobson, Demi Chef. Carina Johnson, Receptionist. James Johnson, Commis Chef. Luke Johnson, Waiter. Zack Jones, Head Kitchen Gardener. Kevin Jones, Kitchen Porter. Mark Jones, Hotel Director. Alan Jones, Gardener. Steff Jones, Deputy GM. Grace Jones, Waiter. Benjamin Jones, Waiter. Isabel Jones, Waiter. Sue Jones, Breakfast Chef. Carolyn Jordan, Room Attendant. Christy Jose, General Assistant. Jack Jowett, Waiter. Harriet Jowett, Waiter. Glenn Joyce, Senior Chef de Partie. Anne Jukes, Room Attendant. Airida Juskeviciute, Events Manager. Louie Jutton, Room Attendant. Rafal Kabasinski, Assistant Head Housekeeper. Emmanouil Kakanas, Senior Chef de Partie. Damla Kaya, Waiter. Ece Kaya, Waiter. Hazel Kayes, Room Attendant. Rachel Keane, Room Attendant. Olivia Keetch, Assistant Reception Manager. Charlotte Keirle, Linen Porter. Jacob Kelly, Senior Sous Chef. Carrington Kelsey-Clark, Housekeeper. Joseph Kenny, Waiter. Sophie Kerslake, Receptionist. Matthew King, Assistant Restaurant Manager. Mary-Beth Kinsey, Reception Office Assistant. Louise Kitching, Therapist. Sophie Kneller, Duty Manager. Thomas Knight - Owen, Bartender. Alexander Knowland, Demi Chef de Partie. Alex Knowles-Mcnab, Group People, Recruitment and Talent Manager. Agnieszka Ksiazek-Jasiorska, Housekeeper. Gabriella Kun, Room Attendant. Natalia Kuna, General Assistant. Sarah Lacey, Receptionist. Jaroslav Lacko, Kitchen Porter. Harrison Landen, Waiter. Clare Lander, Administrator. Ryan Lander, Waiter. Rosana Lander, Assistant Reception Manager. Amie Lankford, Kitchen Porter. Amy Larcombe, Budding Entrepreneur. Craig Lashly, Senior Sous Chef. Nathaniel Last, Waiter. Stephanie Lavill, Senior Therapist. Danielle Law, Assistant Head Receptionist. Libby Lawrence, Receptionist. Amy Lawrie, Waiter. Charlotte Lawson, Waiter. Graham Lay, Room Attendant. Karl Le Roi, Kitchen Porter. Bethan Le Vien, Waiter. Archie Leach, Kitchen Porter. Mark Leahy, Assistant Head Sommelier. Marcus Lee, Assistant Night Manager. Sophie Leedham, Receptionist. Megan Lees, General Assistant. Heather Legg, Breakfast Supervisor. Kieren Legg, Night Porter. Victoria Legg, Therapist. Rosie Lennox, Waiter. Daisy Lenton, Waiter. Peter Lewis, Deputy General Manager. Star Lewis, Junior Assistant Restaurant Manager. Anna Lewis, Breakfast Host. Carol Liddle, Room Attendant. Barbara Ligenza, Housekeeping Supervisor. Sebastian Ligenza, Maintenance Manager. Olivia Lill, Waiter. Magdalena Lis, F&B Manager. Scott Littlejohn, Maintenance Manager. Graham Livingston, Chef de Partie. Leon Lloyd, Breakfast Chef. Ben Lloyd-Jones, Demi Chef de Partie. Pascale Loddo, Head Sommelier. Sophia Loew, Waiter. Grzegorz Lokietek, Assistant Manager. Alana Long, Room Attendant. Sarah Long, Room Attendant. Andrew Longley, Kitchen Porter. Tilly Lynk, Waiter. David Lyons, Kitchen Porter. Jake Mabbutt, Kitchen Porter. Sophie Macdonald, Waiter. Jack Macfarlane, Budding Entrepreneur. Joanna Macina, Group Apiarist. Faye Macklin, Budding Entrepreneur. Isabel Maclaren, Waiter. Tiernan Madgwick, Assistant Head Sommelier. Shannon Madgwick, Reception Manager. Lisa Maggs, Room Attendant. Emanuele Magliocchetti, Kitchen Porter. Valeria Maica, Senior Therapist. Esme Mallett, Receptionist. Daniele Mangini, Assistant Head Sommelier. Shaun Manning, Junior Sous Chef. Alexander Mansfield, Maintenance Manager. Sarah Marchant, Duty Manager. Max Markby Brans, Waiter. Cooper Marlowe, Waiter. Nicolette Marshall, Therapist. Sophie Martineau, Bar Manager. Stuart Mason, Kitchen Porter. Luke Matthews, Waiter. Charlotte Matthews, Receptionist. Louisa Matthews, Commis Chef. Luke Matthews, Kitchen Porter. Thea Mayeux, Waiter. Abigail Mayhew, Receptionist. Emma-Rose Mayne, Head Kitchen Porter. Jolanta Mazurkiewicz, Room Attendant. Philip McCloskey, Night Porter. John McDonald, Breakfast Supervisor. Ella McDonald, Budding Entrepreneur. Sasha McDonald, General Assistant. Eliot Mcgrath, Linen Porter. Charlotte Mcguire, Reservationist. Victoria McIlvenny, Room Attendant. Tara Mclintic, Room Attendant. Kieran McLintic, Maintenance Assistant. Owen McManus, Linen Porter. Emma McNally, Waiter. Philip McNamara, Housekeeping Floor Supervisor. Alexander McNeil, Demi Chef de Partie. Conor McNeil, Waiter. Michael Mead, Night Supervisor. Anna Meehan, Room Attendant. Owen Mellett, Floor Supervisor. Martin Mellor, Chef de Tournant. Vanessa Merrett, Room Attendant. Iona Mesropians, Housekeeping Floor Supervisor. Kate Meyrick, Receptionist. Will Middleton, Waiter. Linda Miles, Room Attendant. Marina Miles, Kitchen Porter. Kirsty Mills, Room Attendant. Jaroslaw Milo, Room Attendant. Petar Minev, Linen Porter. Gemma Mitchell-Mortiboys, Room Attendant. Gabor Molnar, Bar Manager. Fruzsina Molnar, Commis Chef. Charlotte Monk, Waiter. Eleanor Moorcroft, Waiter. Andrew Moore, Senior Head Kitchen Gardener. Gemma Moore, Waiter. Jodie Moore, Waiter. Fiona Moores, Regional Operations Director. Emily Moore-Watts, Room Attendant. Georgie Moretti Shannon, Waiter. Ieaun Morgan, Demi Chef de Partie. Alice Morgan, Room Attendant. Alicia Morley-Blackett, Chef de Rang. Finn Morley-Welch, Bartender. William Morris, Kitchen Porter. Samuel Morris, Waiter. Luigi Morrone, Chef de Partie. Freya Morton, House Manager. Evie Morton, Chef de Rang. Mikael Moussa, Restaurant Manager. Stacey Moxham, Room Attendant. Kelvin Mullins, Group Pastry Trainer. Georgia Mumby, Waiter. Philip Munn, Night Duty Manager. Edward Murphy Jameson, Waiter. Wesley Muzzall, Bartender. Gabriela Nardi, House Manager. Ewa Nasilowska, Assistant Head Sommelier. Robert Neil, Senior Sous Chef. Will Netherway, Reception Supervisor. Natalie Nicholls, Waiter. Sandra Niedzwiecka, Chef de Partie. Bartosz Niedzwiedzki, Chef de Partie. Emma Niven, Waiter. Olivia Nobbs, Waiter. Sherrie-Ann Nolan, Room Attendant. Jeremy Norman, Pastry Chef de Partie. Jessica O'Connor, Waiter. Erin O'Connor, Receptionist. Caitlin O'Connor-Brooke, Bartender. Dellan Oke, Chef de Rang. Grazyna Olbrychowska, Room Attendant. Oliver Oldfield, Bartender. Carlos Oliveira, Room Attendant. Gary Orris, Night Porter. Edward Osborne, Head Sommelier. Kamil Oseka, Head Chef. Gareth Osment, Chef de Partie. Iwona Ostrowska, Deputy Head Housekeeper. Racheal Owen, Room Attendant. Jemima Owen, Waiter. Emeline Owen, Receptionist. James Oxley, Sous Chef. Sacha Palmer, Room Attendant. Khafera Palmer-Benn, Commis Chef. Alvaro Panadero Amado, Breakfast Chef. Philip Papworth, Bartender. Jessica Parker, Reservationist. William Parkes, Senior Sous Chef. Ellis Parkinson, Room Attendant. Stuart Parr, Kitchen Porter. Oscar Parrick, Linen Porter/Room Attendant. Katie Parsons, Reception Manager. Miguel Pascual Sanchez, Chef de Partie. Istvan Patko, Head Sommelier. Emese Patko-Horvath, Pastry Sous Chef. Jessica Pearce, Events Co-Ordinator. Abigail Pearson, Waiter. Samantha Penney, Receptionist. Mark Perry, Head Groundsperson. Bethany Perry, Kitchen Gardener. Sophie Perry, Deputy General Manager. Della Perry, Waiter. Gavin Phillips, Night Manager. Lauren Phillips, Waiter. Natasha Phillips, Waiter. Harry Phillips, Kitchen Gardener.

Sylvi Pickering, Waiter. Annie Pickhaver, Gardener. Joseph Pike, Chef de Partie. Teanna Pilgrim, Waiter. Stephen Pinkney, Kitchen Porter. Simone Pinkney, Floor Supervisor. Julie Pithers, Reservationist. Verity Pitts, Host. Maria Consuelo Platero Moreno, Head Groundsperson. John Plunkett, Night Porter. Jessica Porch, Waiter. Thomas Porch, Apprentice. Jade Porter, Housekeeper. Joe Potter, Junior Sous Chef. Matthew Pottinger, Senior Chef de Partie. Ruth Pound, Assistant Head Housekeeper. Oliver Powell, Receptionist. Teuta Pranic, Therapist. George Price, House Manager. Ruby Price, Waiter. Spencer Price, Waiter. Catherine Price, Events Manager. Jonathan Prikockis, Group Revenue Manager. Jack Pritchard, Assistant Head Sommelier. Alex Proudman, Senior Sous Chef. Lee Pulman, Chef de Rang. Natasha Quinn, Therapist. Rebecca Rackley, Breakfast Chef. Oliver Rainer, Waiter. Emma Rainforth, Kitchen Porter. Jack Ralphs, General Assistant. David Ramos, Groundsperson. Laura Raymond, Therapist. Jonty Read-Ball, Kitchen Porter. Roseanna Reed, Head Kitchen Gardener. Louise Renshaw, Reservation Manager. Claire Renton-Skinner, Chef. Tara Rex, Head Therapist. Kian Rex, Kitchen Porter. Jill Rey-Cambre, Accounts Assistant. David Richards, Night Porter. James Rider, Apprentice. Lydia Rigby, Restaurant Manager. Daniela Ristea, Therapist. Scarlett Roach, Waiter. Helen Roberts, Digital Marketing Manager. Georgia Roberts, Room Attendant. Evie Robertson, Waiter. Rebecca Robinson, Assistant Manager. Andrew Robinson, Night Porter. Beatrice Robinson, Apprentice. Stephen Rockey, Director of People. Lucy Rodham, Therapist. Gina Roe, Head of Payroll. Anthony Rogers, Waiter. Rex Rogers, Waiter. Miguel Rojo, Grounds Assistant. Lottie Rooke - James, Linen Porter/Room Attendant. Lily Rosier, Head Therapist. Tom Ross, Group Operations Director. Billie Ross, Bartender. James Rothnie, Chef de Partie. Emma Roulier, Health & Safety Administrator. Sophie Rout, Waiter. James Rowley, Waiter. Nicholas Rudge, Night Manager. Leanne Rudling, Housekeeping Supervisor. Lucia Rugge-Price, Waiter. Georga Rumph, Room Attendant. Louise Rusca, Junior Assistant Restaurant Manager. Maja Rzepka, Assistant Manager. Caesar Saavedra, Commis Chef. Annabella Sames, Demi Chef de Partie. Dulcie Sanders, Budding Entrepreneur. Penny Sargent, Bartender. Laura Saunders, Receptionist. Elliot Saunders, Senior Chef de Partie. Laurence Saunders, Trainee Sommelier. Jane Scott, Therapist. Nathaniel Scott, Groundsman. Gabriel Scott-Masson, Apprentice. Robin Selman, Apprentice. Sarah Sennett, Reservationist. William Sewell, Bartender. James Shadbolt, Head Chef. Stuart Shaw, Gardener. Charlie Shepherd, Kitchen Porter. June Sherlock, Reservationist. Ben Shorthouse, Bartender. Haydn Shute, Kitchen Apprentice. Zaneta Siedlecka, Night General Assistant. Alfie Siggers, Bartender. Maisie Sillence, Supervisor. Bertina Silva, Assistant Restaurant Manager. Joelle Simpson, Bartender. Anthony Sims, Junior Sous Chef. Benjamin Skedd, Budding Entrepreneur. George Skinner, Waiter. Adrian Slazynski, Assistant Restaurant Manager. Kieran Sleep, Kitchen Porter. Ramunas Sliozevicius, Groundsperson. Camilla Sloan, Budding Entrepreneur. Leslie Smallwood, Kitchen Porter. Eve Smith, Administrator. Charlotte Smith, Management Accountant. June Smith, Room Attendant. Ellen Smith, Therapist. Dom Smith, Waiter. Silas Smith, Bartender. Olivia Smith, Therapist. Grant Solf, Chef de Partie. Maria Joselia Sousa, Room Attendant. Maria Sousa De Jesus, Housekeeping Supervisor. Barbara Sowa, Accounts Assistant. Bonnie Sparks, Payroll Systems Administrator. David Spears, Maintenance. Byron Spence, Kitchen Porter. Benjamin Spilsbury, Commis Chef. Jodie Spring, Receptionist. Minnie Stagg, Receptionist. Jack Stallard, Head Chef. Cristina Stan, Room Attendant. Katarzyna Stankiewicz, Room Attendant. Sebastian Stawarz, Breakfast Chef. Nicola Stedman, Receptionist. Max Stennett, Bar Manager. Lucy Stewart, Accounts Assistant. Kathryn Stewart, Breakfast Supervisor. Nicola Stewart, Chef de Partie. Joseph Stickney, Waiter. Harry Stilwell, Assistant Sommelier. Relu Stochitoiu, Kitchen Porter. Helen Stockall, Kitchen Porter. Liam Stocker, Apprentice. Jacqui Stokes, Long-suffering PA to Robin. Jake Stokes, Waiter. Piotr Stolarek, Linen Porter. Grace Stone, Waiter. William Stone, Bartender. Faye Stone, Administrator. Charlotte Storey, Deputy General Manager. Lora Strizic, Regional Operations Director. Katy Strong, Room Attendant. Alex Sultan, Kitchen Gardener. Christian Summers, Demi Chef de Partie. Namfon Surintraboon, Room Attendant. Jessica Surman, Receptionist. Amber Sutton, Assistant to Judy Hutson. Eliza Swain Thompson, Demi Chef de Partie. Hayley Symonds, Budding Entrepreneur. Rebecca Symons, Recruitment Adviser. Calum Syrett, Bar Supervisor. Robert Tansley, Kitchen Porter. Harry Tarrant, Chef de Partie. Sophie Tattam, Office Manager. Megan Tayler, Head Waiter. Martin Taylor, Night Porter. Patrick Taylor, Kitchen Porter. Michael Tearle, Gardener. Geanina Tene, Head Housekeeper. Stephen Thomas, Night Porter. Henrietta Thomas, Waiter. Lauren Thompson, Receptionist. Nate Thompson, Bartender. Edward Thornton, Kitchen Gardener. Eleanor Thurlby, Waiter. Luke Thurlow, Night Porter. Tom Tillett, Bartender. Desislava Todorova, Room Attendant. Reece Tomkins, Kitchen Porter. Sunny Townsend, Waiter. Laura Trego, Sommelier. Katherine Trenchard, Chef de Rang. Paul Florin Trifanov, Head Kitchen Porter. Rowan Trim, Restaurant Manager. Ravid Tripp, Sous Chef. Jasmine Tritton, Reception Manager. Petar Tsvetanov, Housekeeping Supervisor. Bogomil Tsvetanov, Bartender. Michelle Tucker, Breakfast Manager. Oliver Tucker, Head Chef. Matthew Turner, Maintenance Manager. Gregory Turner-Deeks, Head Sommelier. Daisy Turney, F&B Manager. Angela Tyrrell, Room Attendant. Alfonso Urruti, Deli Manager. Angel Uzunov, Linen Porter. Vanya Uzunova, Floor Supervisor. Sergio Valera Amoros, Chef de Rang. Cadi Van Dyk, Sommelier. Margaret Veale, Room Attendant. Sam Vesey, Bar Manager. Charles Wade, Waiter. Natalie Waite, Reception Manager. Andrew Walford, Kitchen Apprentice. Arran Walton, Events Co-Ordinator. Jack Walton, Kitchen Garden Supervisor. Alice Ward, Receptionist. Lee Ward, Grounds Assistant. Joanna Warner, Administrator. Diane Warner, Room Attendant. Bradley Warren, Trainee Sommelier. Samantha Warren, Restaurant Supervisor. Emma Warren, Waiter. Lewis Watkins, Maintenance. Megan Watkins, Waiter. Adam Watson, Kitchen Porter. Ryan Watts, Waiter. Bethan Way, Group Training & Communications Manager. Megan Way, Assistant Festival Manager. Lesley Weatherill, Therapist. Sarah Wentz, Duty Manager. Timothy Werger, Waiter. Hayley Wetherill, Head Housekeeper. Chelsea Whitcher, Housekeeper. Charlotte Whitcher, Housekeeper. Molly White, Assistant Restaurant Manager. Harry White, Head Sommelier. Olivia White, Therapist. Taegan White, Waiter. Katie Whittle-Penwarden, Assistant Restaurant Manager. Archie Whitton, Kitchen Porter. Sarah Wickins, Waiter. Harvey Wilkins, General Assistant. Dave Wilkinson, IT Business Analyst. Thomas Williams, Senior Chef de Partie. Susan Williams, Room Attendant. Michael Williams, Junior Sous Chef. Tilly Williams, Marketing Assistant. Jeremy Williams, Kitchen Porter. Abigail Williamson, Waiter. Penny Willis, Commis Sommelier. Kristian Willson-Lloyd, Waiter. Christa Wilson, Room Attendant. Isabelle Wilson, Waiter. Maisie Wilson, Waiter. Poppy Winstanley, Junior Sous Chef. Olivia Woodger, Therapist. James Woodward, Maintenance Assistant. Andy Wright, Regional Head Chef. Octavia Wright, Reservationist. Jake Wright, Kitchen Porter. Abby Wrigley, Supervisor. Sarah Yarnall, Executive Housekeeper. Alexis Yarnall, Reception Office Assistant. Krystina Yates, Admin Assistant. Ryan Yates, Maintenance Manager. Steph Young, Floor Manager. Kamil Zachara, Kitchen Porter. Katarzyna Zajac, Deputy Head Housekeeper. Jakub Zajac, Maintenance. Jolanta Zakrzewska, Head Housekeeper. Lukasz Zakrzewski, Maintenance Manager. Joseph Zani, Bartender. Kaci Zarczynski, Bartender. Iwona Zielinska, Housekeeper. Antanas Zorinas, Linen Porter.

Written by Robin Hutson, Gill Morgan, Lex Bartlett-Woodnutt

Photography by John Carey

Illustrations by Will Dozer

Art direction by Sara Redhead

Designer Helen Bratby

Researcher/writer Alex Moore

Recipe copy editor Aggie Mackenzie

Copy editors Natalie Reed, Damon Syson

Project managers Emma Cripwell, Sarah Glyde

Publishing consultant Camilla Leask

First published in Great Britain in 2022 by The Home Grown Hotels

Edited and designed by Uncommonly Ltd

The Pig's charity partners are:
Action Against Hunger; Hospitality Action; Belu Water; Royal Academy of Culinary Arts Adopt a School Trust; Oasis Farm Waterloo; National Lobster Hatchery.

Printed in East Sussex by Pureprint, a CarbonNeutral® Company. The paper is carbon balanced with the World Land Trust, an international conservation charity.

A CIP catalogue record for this book is available from the British Library.

ISBN 978-1-3999-0742-2

BERK
-SHIRE
WILT
-SHIRE
HAMP
-SHIRE
ISLE OF
WIGHT